BUBER AND HUMANISTIC
EDUCATION

Buber and Humanistic Education

by

JOSHUA WEINSTEIN

University of Houston

PHILOSOPHICAL LIBRARY
New York

Copyright, 1975, by
PHILOSOPHICAL LIBRARY INC.,
15 East 40 Street, New York, N. Y. 10016

Library of Congress Catalog Card No. 74-84861
SBN 8022-2157-2

Manufactured in the United States of America

TO RACHEL

INTRODUCTION

The complexity of the places and times in which Martin Buber lived was exceeded only by the intricate societal contrasts by which mankind was then confronted. In Central and Eastern Europe in 1878 and the subsequent decades, rapidly changing economic and political conditions accentuated the instability of life in general and the life of the exploited in particular. And yet, in these times and places, there emerged a unique man whose own quality of life depended for its stability and direction on his ability to synthesize the positive aspects of his total heritage into daily "blueprints for living." Buber continually capitalized on the strength of his religion, his cultural heritage, and his faith in the educability of man as he responded to the challenges and traumas of an ever-changing world. He emerged with a purposefulness that was transmitted to all who understood his messages and found consolation and hope in his teachings.

In the era that Buber lived, the search for solutions to societal weaknesses transcended all barriers and provided the purposes and the patterns for new approaches to self-realization and societal harmony through a synthesized humanistic value system. His philosophic teachings were not new but were ageless enough to challenge the thoughts and actions of those who again witnessed in their own time the inhumanity of man to man. Following in the footsteps of other great philosophic leaders, Buber envisioned the achievement of his humanistic and pansophic goals through education.

Demonstrating an acute sensitivity to the impact of forces for good and evil in the culture to which he was born as well as those with which he learned to live, Buber seemed to live in a constant state of philosophical reassessment. Within the special and temporal limits of his experience, he continued to search for better solutions to the problems of the segments of mankind with which he had intimate acquaintance. He sought his solutions in those cultural constants that knew neither the limits of time nor space. Consequently, one studying his views today in a different time, from vastly different cultural backgrounds, and in an era completely unfamiliar with or to Buber, finds the same basic similarity of problems as many of those he addressed. It is, therefore, possible that by examining his conceptualization of possible solutions, searching minds today may find some elusive thread that can challenge and propel them to expand their understanding of mankind as it struggles to survive and improve.

Educators continue to receive the charge to develop our vast human resources into more effective representatives of humanity. Such responsibilities mandate the examination of every possible source of ideas and processes which may provide clues to the vastness of the task and the complexity of the solutions. Martin Buber devoted his life to coping, assessing, and searching for solutions when confronted in his times and places with responsibilities of similar magnitude and urgency. Educational leaders today are searching for hope, stimulation, and reassurance as they constantly struggle to humanize mankind as dehumanizing odds mount. When conditions discourage teachers from the accomplishment of their goals, the intrinsic relationship of the teacher and the learner depicted by Buber should elevate their hopes and reassure them of the importance of their efforts. When confusion regarding the goals of education distracts our leaders from recognizing the urgency of educating all of our people toward a better quality of life, perhaps awareness of the teachings of Buber would offer clarity and challenge. Perhaps, when the mounting cost of education confounds our economists, the totality of educational impact on both the nation and the world could be brought into new focus by familiarity with the ideas discussed by Martin Buber. Agreement or disagreement with his assessments and interpretations may be of little consequence to today's educational leader. However, awareness of his existence, his ideas, and his teachings affords a rich and rare humanistic experience, the value of which cannot be contested.

Dr. June Hyer
Vice Chancellor and Provost
University of Houston
Clear Lake City

Contents

FOREWORD

THIS BOOK is not a monolith. It is not addressed to just one major issue. It is a compilation of significant educational positions which are contained in the writings of Martin Buber and together comprise his educational theory.

Buber was a great thinker, but he was not an academic philosopher nor a professional educational theoretician. His interests were not directed toward abstract philosophy nor abstract educational theory, but to everyday encounters between man and man. His theories were blueprints for action which aimed not only to bring man into possession of his immediate culture, but also to change man's cultural environment into a climate of equality, harmony, justice and peace. His teachings encouraged the establishment of a pan-human and supernational world society, a messianic era for mankind. He viewed education as the agent whose deliberate task it is to teach youth to investigate wisely and critically what is true and deserves their trust. He believed that the future of mankind lay in eternal-universal values which could forge a diversity of individuals into a cohesive unity, and that education worthy of its name must be directed toward the fostering of a continuous desire for such values. His educational writings were directed toward this goal and the aim of this study is to introduce these teachings of Martin Buber to the educational community.

JOSHUA WEINSTEIN

University of Houston
Houston, Texas
January 1975

ACKNOWLEDGMENT

This book reflects the influence and assistance of several people to whom I am indebted in a special sense. My wife, Rachel, served as a perceptive, critical and demanding critic. Dr. June Hyer, the Provost and Vice Chancellor of the University of Houston at Clear Lake Center, my mentor and friend, wrote the introduction for my book. My good friend, Stanley Epstein, supplied wise comments and edited this manuscript with his fine mind and his professional pen. Professor William Duer of the Houston Baptist University generously offered critical and helpful suggestions. Mrs. Mary San Angelo, sensitive and expressive artist, drew the beautiful picture of Buber for the jacket of my book. Mrs. Jinx Schkade and Mrs. Juanita Maddox, amanuences supreme, prepared the manuscript. To these individuals I extend an author's gratitude.

J. W.

BUBER AND HUMANISTIC
EDUCATION

The Man and His Culture

BUBER'S LIFE was a rich tapestry of conditions and events which paralleled historical movements and ideological schools of thought. He was a product of two great cultures, European, especially German, and Jewish. His intellectual life was affected by the Jewish and the European aspirations and agonies of the last quarter of the nineteenth century and the first half of the present century. Those were turbulent years which were reflected in the optimistic enlightenment of the European culture, the intellectual erudity of the Haskalah, the mystic spirit of the Hasidim, the critical analysis of the German philosophers, the melancholy of two world wars and the messianic hopes which arose with the establishment of Israel as a state. These movements and thoughts left on his soul indelible intellectual marks. Gradually these impressions blended together and consequently emerged as his unique dialogical philosophy. His philosophic genesis was rooted in his particular Jewish traditional heritage; from here he ventured out into the riches of the secular intellectual world; and finally came to rest on his people's universal messianic values. His life and thoughts were intensely interrelated. This interrelationship calls for a study of Buber as a person.

Buber was born in Vienna in 1878. At the age of three the boy's parents became estranged and he went

1

to live in Poland with his grandfather, Solomon Buber, a noted scholar of the Haskalah, the Jewish enlightenment movement. In this home he received a firm grounding in traditional Jewish education. Here he was exposed to the teachings of the two great Jewish movements of that period: the Haskalah and the Hasidut which influenced his future life immeasurably.

Hasidut

Both the Hasidut and the Haskalah movements were products of their times and circumstances. They came to answer the needs of their epochs. They brought solace to yearning hearts and meaning to anguished souls.

Poland of the sixteenth century was one of the largest and most powerful states in Europe, but two centuries later it was reduced to a weak and most vulnerable state which was slated to death. The country drifted to political chaos and economic bankruptcy. The Jews of Poland, who in the sixteenth century had been the elite of the world Jewry, declined by the eighteenth century in strength and stature. In the middle of the seventeenth century, Bodgen Chmielnicki, with his insurrectionist Ukraine army, swept Poland and murdered tens of thousands of Jews. Soon after, the devastating rule of the Saxon kings ensued. Licentious nobles claimed ownership to the land and the labor of the Polish serfs and robbed the possessions and earnings of the Jews. When social unrest engulfed the Polish peasantry, their wrath was shrewdly vented against the Jews, who were libelled by the Polish fanatic clergy as "Killers of Christ." The result was pogrom and massacre.

The latter half of the eighteenth century brought political, economic and cultural disaster to Poland. In 1792 the troops of Russia and Prussia moved into Poland, Lithuania, and Ukraine. Prussia annexed greater Poland, and Russia expropriated substantial parts of Lithuania and the Ukraine. The Polish government became para-lyzed, destroying what little remained of Jewish security. The lives of the Jews were now reduced to the status of pariahs. Their source of livelihood was cut off and their existence depended on menial labor, peddling and hawk-ing. With their political and economic security having collapsed, they turned to their ancient religion for solace and comfort. Alas, their traditional theologies and litur-gies could not give them spiritual comfort. They were too sophisticated, too classical, and too rational. They employed a dialectical technique which bordered on sophistry. They lacked the warmth and the rich moral and ethical significance which Judaism so desperately needed. They were devoid of the spiritual consolation for their anguished people.[1] During those days scholar-ship declined and melancholy overtook Jewish life. As an antidote to this melancholy and despair came a new movement, the Hasidut, and its adherents the Hasidim.

Buber came to know Hasidut, the movement which so greatly influenced his later development, during his tender years, while he stayed in his grandfather's house. This was a movement which had its origins in the ham-lets, small towns and villages of Eastern Europe; Ukraine and Poland. It was established in the eighteenth century by the afflicted Jews who, in their despair, awaited the coming of their Messiah but instead saw the coming of the Cossacks, pogroms and persecutions. It was a move-ment which advocated complete confidence in God and realization that His presence is everywhere. If God is always present, the Hasidim reasoned, why be afraid?

3

Consequently man should always be joyous. Man needs only to fulfill God's commandments with joy and devotion and he will find his realization.

Even if man is not learned and even when he errs out of ignorance or weakness, his prayer is accepted because God values man's inner spirit and good intentions. Like the Christian evangelical sects—the Shakers, Baptists and Dunkards—they emphasized new birth, illumination, animation, song and inner emotionalism. It was a religion of emotions and feelings, an innovated religion. It spoke to the heart. It fused mysticism and ritualism. It believed in spiritual healing through prayer and divine thoughts. It emphasized the importance of worship of God through prayer, joy, ecstatic elation of the soul and personal devotion. Being poor and ignorant, the Hasidim professed contempt for intellectualism, particularly Talmudic erudition. They held that one could find fulfillment only in the world of the spirit. In this world of the spirit all are equal: rich and poor, literate and illiterate. They professed faith in the coming of the messiah whose arrival can be hastened through personal inner devotion, prayer, song, dance and joy. Theirs was a community of true brotherhood where each Hasid was ready, without reservations, to give his life for his fellow Jew. This movement offered not only a life of joy and spiritual security, but it also instilled in its adherants a sense of equality and responsibility for one another.[2] True, the Hasidim whom Buber knew were pale shadows of their ancestors, the great Hasidic masters like the Baal Shem Tov and his early disciples, but Buber was still able to capture their spirit and their creative communal life. Although his early encounter with the Hasidic movement could not win him over completely, he later returned to it as a model and a source of inspiration. The influence of this movement which emphasized happiness and joyful worship of God in the here-and-now world, impressed him for life. Its impact on him was so great that he withdrew in 1904 from his active life to study their teachings which he later published in impressive rhapsodic style in his famous book, "The Tales of the Hasidim."

Haskalah

During his childhood, Buber encountered yet another great movement which affected his life considerably. This was a movement of scholarship, modernism and enlightenment, one which returned to the Jew the sense of self-esteem, dignity and freedom. This was the throbbing activity which, in time, gave birth to the free, democratic and modern State of Israel and the liberal, ambitious and creative Israeli. To this program of Jewish Enlightenment was assigned the name Haskalah.

Throughout the history of mankind, small groups of very influential individuals have shaped and altered the course of human affairs-such as the artists of the Italian Renaissance, the writers of Elizabethan England and the philosophers of eighteenth century France. In the nineteenth century such a minority made its appearance among the Jews of Eastern Europe and established the Haskalah-the period of Jewish Enlightenment. It was powerful in its impact. It revolutionized and modernized Jewish thoughts and behavior. It made Jewish living meaningful and purposeful and served as a turning point in Jewish history.

Until the Haskalah, Eastern European Jewish life was provincial, dreary, and bordered on narrow pietism. The

Jews often lived, as we have seen, a degenerating and unproductive life of petty trade and vocational marginalism. They lost their self respect and human dignity. In this atmosphere the Haskalah appeared as a beacon of light. It gave purpose to their lives and hope for a better tomorrow.

The intellectual awakening among the Jews paralleled the cultural enlightenment of the East European secular society. While West Europe was awakened by the Renaissance and the French Revolution, East Europe came to life only after the Congress of Vienna in 1815, following the defeat of Napoleon. The Congress resulted in increased trade between East and West and brought illumination to Eastern Europe. Merchants and men of affairs visited France and Germany and learned of Western science, energy, liberalism, social structure and political systems. So impressed were they with what they saw, that they set out to incorporate into the Russian system their newly acquired Western theories and techniques.

Western life soon made its impression on the Jewish communities of Russia and Poland. The Jews were among the early traders with Western Europe and were much impressed with the Western culture and its way of life. The results were revolutionary. The Maskilim, the Haskalah scholars, broke out of their intellectually stagnant ghettos and vigorously embarked on the path of humanism, scholarship, equality, and emancipation. They urged their fellow Jews to integrate into the secular world community while holding on steadfast to their Jewish tenets and principles. They set out to master the German and Russian languages and to gain proficiency in the arts and the sciences of the progressing secular world. They also encouraged their fellow Jews to become

6

economically productive and to assume useful and dig-
nified livelihoods. They promoted secular scholarship
which they believed would gain them greater dignity and
respect from their gentile neighbors. Samson Block enun-
ciated a major purpose of the movement when he said
that the Haskalah removed "the shame of ignorance and
the disgrace of idleness and poverty."

The Maskilim, on the whole, remained observant and
devoted Jews while applying their secular knowledge
and skills towards the betterment of their cultural and
economic life. They applied humanism to their personal
lives as well as scholarship. The trend in the Haskalah
was toward Hebrew letters as a fine arts and a break
from the dogma of rabbinism. The study of their glorious
ancient past awakened in their hearts and minds a national spirit and a hope for repatriation to their ancient
homeland. This spirit of the Haskalah quest for knowledge left a lasting mark on Buber.[3] Together with the
Hasidic zeal and fervor, it later culminated in his social
humanistic concerns and his prophetic universal hopes.

Secular Intellectualism

At the age of fourteen, Buber left his grandfather's
home to study at the gymnasium of Lemberg and the
universities of Berlin and Vienna.

Western Europe of that era was permeated with new
cultural and intellectual currents and Buber ventured
into this world in search for knowledge, meaning and
direction. Like other young people of this era he absorbed vast accumulated traditional knowledge in philosophy, art and science. But he soon became disenchanted.
The conventional European philosophies did not touch

his soul, nor did they give him direction. The only movement which truly affected him and transformed him into a universalist and humanist was the relatively new school of thought and approach to life-the existential philosophy.

Existentialism was the new intellectual child of that era and culture. It was nurtured in the eighteenth century after two great revolutions, the French and the American. This was a time when men everywhere were denouncing dogma, corruption, and ignorance. Man was seeking new and relevant values. He rejected the external and supernatural values which were impressed on his society. He searched for values which were the product of his own creative thinking and could satisfy his contemporary needs. The entire Western world was permeated with the spirit of rational skepticism and searched for new and greater humanism and enlightenment. The dominant intellectual force at that time were the French Philosophers, who together with the Industrial Revolution set out to remake society from a static feudal order into a competitive, laissez-faire structure whose political controls passed into the hands of the masses. Rather than await compensation in the unknown Kingdom of Heaven, Nietzsche, the nineteenth century philosopher, proclaimed that God is dead and suggested that man orient himself toward joy and satisfaction in the world of here and now. But neither did the physical world nor the pleasures of the contemporary society satisfy man.

The political strife and conflicts of the nineteenth century soon turned man's skepticism into depressive passivism and apprehension. For a while it was hoped that the methods employed by scientists in the natural-physical world would solve man's personal and social problems, but no panacea was found even in the modern inventions. Social science too failed. The social experimentations which were designed to make people happy and content resulted in disappointment and dissatisfaction. Neither did theological and philosophical absolutes nor scientific formulas bring happiness nor inner satisfaction to man. They did not alleviate human suffering, uncertainty and absurdity, simply because these external devices did not have it within their power to do so.[4]

But man need not go far to search for solutions to his problems, claimed the existentialists who profoundly influenced Buber. They claimed that the solution lies within man himself. Man need not look for purpose in our universe, because the universe has no purpose. It is only man who has purpose and the meaning for man's life is to be found within man himself. So it is with truth. It is not absolute and does not reside outside of man. Truth can be found only within man himself, within his feelings, within his situation, within his soul.[5] This is also true with reality. The real world is not the ideal nor the abstract world. It is our existing World, the world of today. It is the world in which we are authentically involved; the world which we directly experience; and the world with which we directly interact.

A major influence on Buber was the German philosopher, Friedrich Nietzsche, whom Buber regarded as the first pathfinder of the new culture of his era. From Nietzsche he learned to emphasize what is concrete and actual, creative and dynamic. Although he abhored Nietzsche's concepts of "Will to Power" and "Superman," he cherished his existential and humanistic views which aimed to promote the supremacy of man.

9

Nietzsche insisted on man's inalienable right for freedom and self actualization. He refuted Kantian morality and the concept of Categorical Imperative. Human beings, he claimed, can not be added up like things, and truth can not be an abstraction which is accepted by all human beings. Truth is subjective and not at all inclusive. Truth depends on the unique person and the unique situation.[6]

Nietzsche rejected industrial capitalism as an instrument which leads to dehumanization of society because it standardizes man's life, it establishes routine, it levels all people, and evaluates man quantitatively rather than treat him as a person. Nietzsche believed that industrial capitalism will cause ultimate demise of culture and art, the two major elements which advance man's dynamism and creativity. Through art and culture man remolds, redirects and reinterprets his world. Both are highly personal and subjective, and must be kept free. Nietzsche insisted on an atmosphere of freedom, and denounced superimposed values. Life must be unbounded and left to man's interpretation.[7]

He interpreted freedom to mean individual freedom toward self actualization, and strongly objected to "equal" rights to all, which in his opinion levels the entire society, depersonalizes individuals and deprives talented persons of their opportunity for excellence. He expressed disdain of any form of collective behavior and insisted on man's right for uninhibited development and self expression. The better educated and the better talented must not be lost in the anonymity of man's schooling.[8]

He objected to mass education. He criticized the schools of his time by stating that, "It is the best teachers . . . who are now perhaps the least fitted, in view of

10

the present standing of our public schools, for the education of select youths, huddled together in a confused heap."[9] As a result of this situation all the students are deprived of a greater intimacy and direct communication between teacher and student. Our schools became dehumanized and depersonalized.

Nietzsche also rejected norms. "The distinguished type of human being feels himself as value determining. It does not need to be ratified; he judges that what is harmful to me is harmful as such . . . The distinguished soul has reverence for himself."[10]

Man must determine his own actions. As a stage manager he must learn to handle his environment, and manipulate with passion and personal trust his entire human scene.[11]

He considered science to be no more than a tool in service of man and held that "a specialist in science gets to resemble nothing but a factory workman who spends his whole life in turning one particular screw or handle or a certain instrument or machine." What counts most is man himself and not the profession which he holds.

Nietzsche's existential views had profound influence on Buber, but so did the views of Soren Kierkegaard, the Danish nineteenth century philosopher who is considered as the progenitor of existentialism.

From Kierkegaard he learned that every person must seek his own pathway to God, and that building faith in God on sheer historical grounds is a fatal delusion.[12] Faith is not expressed in dogma, nor in purely philosophic lines. Faith must provide a substratum of real feelings and emotions.[13]

From Kierkegaard he also learned that man's cherished possession is freedom and that man's freedom involves a

11

"life of toil and much suffering and many dangers." Our worldly lot is danger, suffering and toil. Man attempts to free himself from the tribulations of this world through religious escape, cultural escape, and social escape. But man in search of freedom need not escape from himself. To escape into a collective, be it social, political, or religious, does not extricate man, but leads him to further enslavement-this time to the collective itself. Man need not search far for freedom. He need not venture into the world of dogma nor the collective. He need only look into himself, for there his freedom resides.

Just like freedom, the foundations of morality too lie within man. In order to validate his beliefs man need not turn to social or supernatural proof but to his own inner experiences.[14]

Kierkegaard and Nietzsche nurtured Buber's thirsty soul, but it was Buber himself who ultimately sifted and distilled his accumulated wisdom and formulated his own philosophical anthropology and his unique dialogical philosophy.

Zionism

Although greatly influenced by secular scholarship Buber could not find in it solace for his restless soul. After several years of estrangement he reverted back to Judaism through a new life setting, through Zionism, the movement which aimed to restore dignity to the Jews by restoring them to their ancient homeland.

Zionism was not a unique political creation. Europe of the nineteenth century was laden with progressive self-liberation movements. The genesis of these movements had its roots in modern romanticism. Poets and authors kindled in the hearts of the general population an appreciation for cultural and spiritual heritage. They promoted in the masses a yearning for ethnic music and art, history and folkways. This appreciation for cultural heritage was soon translated into aspirations for self-emancipation and national liberation.

Such aspirations existed within the European Jewish community. The Jewish national movement, too, could be traced to its rich and colorful folklore, to its scholars and poets who rejuvenated through the Haskalah movement, pastoral glories of ancient Israel. They encouraged European Jews to return to the soil of their land and kindled in them a desire to re-establish Israel as a sovereign state. Before the Haskalah vanished in the rubble of the First World War, it gave birth to Zionism, its cultural and political offspring. By holding up the mirror of the glorious Jewish past the Haskalah leaders succeeded in making European Jews realize the sordidness of their present. It kindled in them the desire not only to survive, but to search for a better life ahead, a new horizon. The Haskalah intellectuals who rejected the degrading state of Jewish affairs outlined an idealistic blueprint for a fresh and challenging future. Rather than rely on the mercy of the world or the coming of a mystic messiah, they assumed the responsibility of restoring the Jews to their ancient homeland and their homeland to its ancient political and cultural glory. They maintained that Jews can no longer survive by fleeing anti-semitism from land to land in the hopes of rescue. They resolved to secure the Jewish future through self reliance in a country of their own. They manifested their goal to create for the Jewish people a homeland in Palestine secured by public law. The Jewish romantics of the Haskalah sang the songs of Zion and with fervor echoed:

13

"March forward, Jews of all lands." Moses Hess, the practical statesman of that period called out: "The ancient homeland of yours is calling you, and we will be proud to open its gates for you. March forward, ye sons of martyrs! The harvest of experience which you have accumulated in your long exile will help to bring again to Israel the splendor of the Davidic days and rewrite that part of history of which the monoliths of Semiramis are the only witness."[15]

What intensified the urgency of Jewish statehood was the revival of pogroms in 1880. Spurred by these purgings, many young Jews not only joined Jewish self-defense units but saw in Jewish nationalism the only answer to the new anti-semitic terror. Dr. Leon Pinsker, a theoretical leader of the Haskalah movement reached this conclusion: "Nations live side by side in a state of relative peace, which is based chiefly on the fundamental equality between them . . . but it is different with the people of Israel. This people is not counted among the nations, because since it was exiled from its land it has lacked the essential attributes of nationality, by which one nation is distinguished from another. True, we have not ceased even in the lands of our exile to be spiritually a distinct nation; but this spiritual nationality so far from giving us the status of a nation in the eyes of other nations, is the very cause of their hatred for us as a people. Men are always terrified by a disembodied spirit, a soul wandering about with no physical covering; and terror breeds hatred."[16] Pinsker believed that the Jewish people had to be transformed into a physical formulation in their ancient land—Israel.

The architect of practical Zionism was Theodore Herzl, a Hungarian Jewish journalist, in whose soul echoed the cry of the French mob during the infamous Dreyfus Affair, "Death to the Jews." With the zeal of the prophets of old, supported by the yearnings of his people for redemption, he turned the messianic longing for a return to Zion into a massive political force which ultimately brought his dream to fruition.[17] In his famous pamphlet, "DER JUDENSTAAT," The Jewish State, he proclaimed: "The idea which I have developed in this pamphlet is a very old one. It is the restoration of the Jewish state. The world resounds with outcries against the Jews, and these outcries have awakened this slumbering idea." Herzl's political purpose was to establish a state as an answer to anti-semitism. It did not occur to him, however, that the Jewish affinity to Zion and its cultural tradition were just as valid reasons to establish the state.

Herzl's political Zionism influenced Martin Buber, but his true Zionist mentor was Ahad Ha-Am, who served as the spiritual conscience of Jewish nationalism. Ahad Ha-Am was the pen name of Asher Ginzberg, a Ukrainian Jewish scholar, who was disturbed by the emphasis of Zionism upon the physical rebuilding of Israel as a place of refuge and safety for the Jews. The Jews, he argued, were indeed a nation, but one which depended more on bonds of culture than on territory. He insisted that Jewish nationalism must concern itself with reviving the cultural and spiritual productivity of the Jewish people. He believed that the task of Zionism was to solve not only the problem of the Jew but Judaism as well, and Judaism, according to Ahad Ha-Am, was primarily a spiritual phenomena. He believed that the Jewish will to live was more than a desire for mere survival. It always aimed to create a specific type of life

15

and a specific outlook on human problems. While the Greeks looked for spiritualized materialism, such as expression in beauty of form and language, the Jews looked to the spiritual in the form of discovery of fundamental truth in actual life. The Hebrew spirit was the spirit of values. It did not express itself through physical empires and political institutions, nor through the production of works of art. It manifested itself in the search for righteousness, equality, justice and scholarship. On these qualities it desired to establish a social order of panhuman and super-national dimension. The prophets of ancient Israel insisted on truthfulness, refusal to compromise on principles and perfect justice that leads to truth in action, and thus to righteousness. Judaism considered these utterances on social justice and the ideal conduct of man as the blueprint of its model society.

Ahad Ha-Am viewed Zionism as a movement based on these prophetic principles, a movement in which the individual disregards his personal interest or convenience and does what is right from the point of view of the whole.[18] He demanded that Israel, as a state, become an elemental force which stands for righteousness, justice and equality not only for its own citizens but for all mankind. In short he viewed Zionism as a movement whose task it was to solve not only the political but primarily the spiritual and cultural problems of the Jewish people. He held that the purpose of the new state was to unite the Jewish people through a cultural center and that only the Land of Israel, their ancestral cultural center, could serve such a function. As Israel Friedlander summed it up, "according to Ahad Ha-Am, Zionism must begin with culture and end with culture, its consummation being a center for Judaism."[19]

Buber's Zionism was that of Ahad Ha-Am. He, too, strove for a cultural and intellectual center for world Jewry. Like Ahad Ha-Am he envisioned Judaism as a global civilization from which the Jewish cultural genius would flow into its center, Israel, and from there back into the Jewish communities the world over, thus achieving a universal cultural Jewish unity.

Buber led a rich and active life. In 1916 he became the editor of "Der Jude," a journal of foremost expressions of serious Jewish thinking. In 1923 he accepted an appointment to the chair of Jewish philosophy at the University of Frankfort. At that time he translated the Old Testament, together with Franz Rosenzweig, into German. In 1938 he went to Israel to assume the chair in social philosophy at the Hebrew University. He taught, lectured and wrote. His bibliography contains over 850 items of works which were published in various languages.

The crucible of the intellectual, cultural and political currents forged Buber into an intellectual giant who was viewed in his own life time as a modern sage and prophet. He was acknowledged by Christian and Jewish scholars as one of the most outstanding modern day philosophers and theologians. His existential philosophy influenced philosophers, theologians, educators, sociologists, psychiatrists, psychologists, poets and even political statesmen. Dag Hammarskjold, the United Nations Secretary-General said of him:

> "One can accept his formula as the expression of an extremely fertile philosophy of life and can understand how influential it has become. It has touched on a mystical pantheism, while it still returns the depth and dream of the dualistic relationship with the divine. . . .

17

"Summing up the importance of Buber the philosopher . . . he has been fruitful and inspiring through his philosophical writings in spheres intimately connected with poetry. Further, on the basis of his philosophy, as a shaper of opinion, he has become one of those who has most eloquently defended those forms of contact between people which poetry wants to serve."[20]

The Dialogical Philosophy

UNLIKE OTHER EXISTENTIALISTS, Martin Buber treated education as a serious topic for inquiry. His educational thoughts constitute a unique theory of education. They are founded on his philosophical anthropology and his dialogical philosophy and therefore can not be treated in isolation. In order to understand his significant educational theories in their proper perspective it is necessary to review briefly his "I-Thou" concept which is the heart of his dialogical philosophy.

I and Thou

Buber's entire philosophy was built on the concept of unity. Man's greatest achievement in life, he claimed, is the attainment of unity: unity within the single man, unity between man and man, unity among the segments of a nation, unity among nations, unity between mankind and the inanimate world, and unity between the universe and God. This unity is basically spiritual in nature and is achieved by building spiritual bridges between man and man, between man and nature, and between man and his spiritual world. He proposed his "I-Thou" dialogue as an instrument for the attainment of this unity.

What is the "I-Thou" dialogical concept?

19

Bergman[21] introduced a simplified theory of Kant as a means to explain Buber's dialogical concept. Our world and everything in it, explained Kant, is bi-polar. A subject is a subject in relationship to an object, and an object is an object in relationship to a subject. There is no subject without an object and there is no object without a subject. It is the relationship between the two which makes the subject and the object what they are. So it is with Buber's theory. What really exists between man and man, man and nature, and man and his spiritual world is a relationship, or more correctly, an attitude.

Buber spoke of two primary attitudes between man and his surrounding world: the "I-Thou" and the "I-It" attitudes. The basic words "I," "Thou," and "It," he explained, come in pairs, in which the two words relate to each other. The word "I" does not exist by itself nor do the words "Thou" and "It." They are intertwined into an "I-Thou" or an "I-It" relationship. In order to accentuate the special meaning of these relationships, Buber deliberately ignored the common word "you" and instead introduced the word "Thou," which represents in his vocabulary uniqueness and significance. By using the word "Thou," he wished to connote presentness, mutuality, directness, familiarity and ineffability. He wished to connote the familiarity, mutuality and inclusiveness which exist between a living mother and her beloved child, between husband and wife in the passion of merged feelings and understanding, where the common word "you" does not suffice, and the personal familiar "Thou" is required to indicate a binding relationship and an attitude of communion. The "I-Thou" attitude represents the supreme level of relationship

20

which is exemplified through authentic communion and loss of consciousness.

While "I-Thou" is dialogue, "I-It" is monologue. "I-It" is one sided, relating to man's confined physical and empirical world, to the world of things, to the world of use and experience. The "I-It" is a subject-object relationship. It is an attitude which is always indirect and treats even people as objects. This is a theory void of mutuality and communion.

The world which is composed of an "I-It" philosophy is totally different from the world which is founded on an "I-Thou" relationship. The world of the "I-It" is a world where man exists at the side of objects and where one object exists at the side of another object. A table, a chair, a pencil, an eraser, and even a messenger boy who happens to pass through an office are no more than things which happen to exist side by side without inter-relationship and without mutuality with the person who happens to occupy the office. Theirs is a mere "I-It" relationship and no more.

Not so with the mother who firmly clasps in her shaking hands the cardboard picture of her beloved son who is away at war, or the frightened little girl who clutches in her hands her cherished rag doll and stares straight into its glass eyes begging for protection and comfort. In these cases, the cardboard picture is not an image and the rag doll is indeed not an object. Both exist and are vividly alive in the eyes of their beholders. The picture and the doll are no "Its." They are both "Thou" incarnate. They respond to those who address them just like all concerned people who are real and affectionate and alive.[22]

Victor Frankel, in his book "Man's Search for Meaning"[23] told a stirring anecdote which depicts a true "I-Thou" attitude: A young woman who was stricken with a terminal disease knew that she was about to die in a few days. Yet, in spite of this knowledge, she was happy and cheerful. Pointing through her window at a tree she said: "This tree here is the only friend I have in my loneliness. I often talk to this tree." Frankel was startled and did not quite know how to take her words. He asked her if the tree replied. "Yes" she answered with conviction. "And what did the tree say?" inquired Frankel. The woman did not hesitate. "It said to me— I am here, I am life, eternal life."

The importance of the above story lies in one's attitude. To Frankel, the tree was no more than an "It," an inanimate object occupying space and time outside a window. To the sick woman, the tree was a "Thou," an intimate living being, with whom she maintained a personal mutual attitude, communicating with it as she would to a dear and responding person.

"I-Thou" is man's supreme relationship but the melancholy of our fate dictates that while the "It" need not become a "Thou" at all, the "Thou" cannot forever remain a "Thou," no matter how exclusively present the "Thou" is in the direct relationship. "I" maintains with "Thou" only fleeting glances. The "Thou" continually becomes an "It" and the "It" may only occasionally become a "Thou" again. Buber presented an example of such a relationship between the "I" and "Thou": A child, lying in its bed with half closed eyes, waits with a tense soul for its mother to speak to it, anxiously desires to communicate with her. The mother arrives, they glance at each other, their eyes shining with love. This, to Buber, is an experience of communion and mutuality.

But this communion and mutuality is short lived, lasting for a moment or two. Soon the same child views its mother just like any other object. Now the child no more calls her and neither does the mother answer. The "Thou" has been replaced by the "It."

Man can choose to live entirely in the world of "It" and forever securely do so, but the consequence of this choice is pathetic—man ceases to be man.

Buber explained that the "I-Thou" relationship exists in all realms of life and demonstrated its significance with examples from our three worlds-the world of nature, the world of people, and the world of the intellect. His theories of education take on added import as each of these worlds is examined.

Between Man and Nature

We have seen in Frankel's story how an ordinary tree, a mere object in nature, was transformed into an animated living being. The attitude between the woman and the tree became real and mutual, and the tree turned, from the woman's point of view, into a "Thou." For her, this was not an allegory but a living dialogue with a phenomenon in nature. Mentally receptive for this encounter, she accepted the inanimate object as a "Thou."

Buber's autobiography relates another example of a dialogue with nature. He tells of spending a summer vacation, as a child, on his grandfather's estate, stealing into the stable and gently stroking the neck of a broad dapple-gray horse. "It was not a casual delight," Buber wrote, "but a great, certainly friendly, but also deeply stirring happening. If I am to explain it now, beginning from the very fresh memory of my hand, I must say that what I experienced in touch with the animal was the Other, the immense otherness of the Other, which, however, did not remain strange like the otherness of the ox or the ram, but rather let me draw near and touch it. When I stroked the mighty mane, sometimes marvelously smooth-combed, at other times just as astonishingly wild, and felt the life beneath my hand, it was as though the element of vitality not akin to me, palpably the other, not just another, really the Other itself: and yet it let me approach, confided itself to me, placed itself elementally in the relation of *Thou* and *Thou* with me. The horse, even when I had not begun by pouring oats for him into the manger, very gently raised his massive head, ears flicking, then snorted quietly, as a conspirator gives a signal meant to be recognizable only by his fellow-conspirator; and I was approved." Buber describes how the beautiful "I-Thou" relationship with the horse ceased when once, while stroking the animal, he felt the fun this motion gave him. It was as though he were using and taking advantage of the horse for his own benefit, and instantly his beloved "Thou" became an "It." "The game went on as before," he recalled "but something had changed, it was no longer the same thing. And the next day, after giving him a rich feed, when I stroked my friend's head he did not raise his head. A few years later, when I thought back to the incident, I no longer supposed that the animal had noticed my defection. But at the time I considered myself judged."[24]

Buber maintained that matter in nature can "tell" us something and conduct dialogue with us but he certainly did not propose that a horse or a tree can ever become an "I." The tree can tell something to the woman in the Frankel story and become her "Thou," but the woman can never become a "Thou" to the tree because it lacks the independence and the living consciousness which is the property of man only. It is man's possession of self consciousness and independence which qualifies only him for the role of "I."

Between Man and Man

We saw how an object in nature, such as a tree or a horse, could be treated as a "Thou" with an attitude of communion and inclusion. But just as a man could treat a tree as a "Thou" so could the same man treat a fellow man as an object, with disconcern, just as an "It." A case in point is a doctor-patient relationship. A doctor who projects himself into his patient with concern and affection, and feels his pain and sorrow, says "Thou" to his patient, but when the same doctor treats a patient as a "case" among many other cases he regards him no more than an "It." It's the different attitudes of the doctor to his two patients that Buber refers to as the "in between."

Buber explained the "in betweeness" with an example of love. Love, he said, is not a subjective feeling which lies within people but between them. When a man and a woman are in love, love exists between them, for love is an "in between" attitude. "Feelings dwell in man: but man dwells in love. That is no metaphor, but the actual truth. Love does not cling to the "I" . . . but love is in between "I" and "Thou." The man who does not know this, with his very being know this, does not know love."[25] So it is with all human relations. The real substance of our world is what exists between man and man, namely, attitude. The attitude is either "I-Thou," where the "in between" is mutuality and communion, or "I-It,"

25

where the "in between" consists of void and nothingness. Said Buber: "If I face a human being as my 'Thou'
and say the primary word 'I-thou' to him, he is not a
thing among things and does not consist of things . . . he
is 'Thou' and fills heaven".[26]

The difference is quite pronounced between the world
of "Thou" from the world of "It," but obviously the
world of "I" changes correspondingly in accordance
with its relationship. Buber writes: "The 'I' of the
primary word 'I-Thou' is a different 'I' from that of the
primary word 'I-It.' The 'I' of the primary word 'I-It'
makes its appearance as an individuality and becomes
conscious of itself as subject (of experiencing and using).
The 'I' of the primary word 'I-Thou' makes its appearance as person and becomes conscious of itself as subjec-
tivity (without a dependent genetive) . . . The one is
the spiritual form of natural detachment, the other, the
spiritual form of natural solidarity of connexion."[27] In
the final analysis what determines human relations is the
attitude between man and man.

Between Man and His Creative World

Buber also talked of a third world of attitudes: The
creative world, the world of art in all its manifestations.
This world too is bipolar and lends itself to an "I-Thou"
or an "I-It" relationship. Creativity, he explained, does
not reside in the firmament above us nor does it dwell
within us awaiting fruition. Creative thoughts and artistic concepts are not our subjective creations. Creativity is just another form of dialogue. Man, he explained,
is surrounded by forms which lend themselves to be
shaped and molded into artistic creations. It is as if the

matter steps up to man and asks him to exercise his effective power upon it. It is up to man to treat matter either as a "Thou" or as an "It." If he speaks the primary word out of his being to the form which appears, then the effective power streams out, and the work arises. As with attitude to man and nature, he who speaks the primary word, "Thou," in the creative sense speaks it with his whole being. "The primary word can only be spoken with the whole being. He who gives himself to it may withhold nothing to himself."[28] He is being merged to one with his creation. Alas, just as with attitude to man and nature, once the primary word "I-Thou" has been spoken, the "Thou" turns again into an "It," a thing among things, able to be experienced and described as a sum of quantities only.

Free Will and Predestination

In order to understand Buber's educational ideas in their proper perspective, one must become acquainted with his metaphysical concept of free-will and predestination which he discussed in the second part of his book "I and Thou." Bergman, his colleague and close friend, explained Buber's unique position concerning man's freedom which extends beyond the classical philosophic division of determinism and indeterminism. The determinist says, explained Bergman, that the world is bound to absolute causes which permit no exception, and even man's will is no more than a link in the chain of causes. On the other hand, the indeterminist attempts to prove that the causal chain is not as tight as the determinist assumes it to be, and that there is still room for man's free decisions. Buber, however, viewed this issue from a totally different perspective. The world of "Its," he explained, is the world of nature and science and evolves in an endless chain of causes and effects. Man lives in this world of "Its" and interacts with it. But this is not man's only world. Man is able to relieve himself of the world of cause and effect and bring himself into a world of "I" and "Thou," where the "I" and the "Thou" face each other in complete freedom. Man is capable of elevating himself out of the world of things into a world of free mutuality and attitude. The world of fate and the world of freedom exist side by side and it is man who determines which world to make his own. The choice is his and his alone. When he permits the world of things to rule him, he becomes passive and submissive, a mere link in the chain of cause and effect, but when he elevates himself into the world of mutuality, into the world of "I" and "Thou," both the "I" and the "Thou" exercise their ultimate freedom in spite of the causal world in which they live.[29]

Some philosophers claimed that man's fate is predetermined. Others, like Schopenhauer, advised us to exercise our free will and free ourselves of the world, which, to us, looks genuine, but in reality is inconsequential, bordering on nothingness. Buber disagreed with both these positions. He did not dismiss the world as inconsequential nor subscribe to a predetermined existence. He believed that it is man's task to elevate himself above the material world but at the same time search for freedom through the world itself. "Let us truly love the world with all its horror," says Buber, "let us dare embrace it with our spiritual arms, and then our arms will meet the arms which strengthen it, the arms of God."[30]

The Process of Education

AT THE Third International Pedagogical Conference, held in Heidelberg, Germany, in 1925, Martin Buber delivered an address on education. This address has been considered both by his contemporaries and by modern educators a classic in educational theory and of universal importance. Both this talk and his subsequent discourses on education were received by educators with great enthusiasm because a bridge which never existed before, that between Existentialism and Education, was spanned. This was the first time that an existential philosopher treated education as a serious topic for philosophic inquiry.

The new philosophic movement, existentialism, drew considerable attention in the beginning of the present century, for it provided man with a new perspective of himself, of nature and of God. The new movement also presented new interpretations of freedom and a new outlook on human relations. Education, however, was excluded from these deliberations, excluded because of the very nature of existentialism itself.

To the existentialist, in contrast to all other philosophers, man's existence precedes his essence. Man finds himself in an existing world, not knowing whence he came nor where he is heading. Because he lacks this proof, man cannot accept a pre-defined essence and must

29

claim the right for pure unrestricted freedom to search for truth. His route must be ultimate free-choice and self-determination, and his final reality can be found only by himself and within himself.

In consequence of such freedom, man's relationship with society becomes impractical, and genuine human relationships an impossibility. Based on this approach to life "we might even conclude that existentialism would have no traffic with education in any shape or form. Indeed the case might even develop that existentialism is the very denial of education as we understand it today."[31] Small wonder that existentialism made little, if any, inroads into American public education.

Martin Buber emerged as a notable and noticeable exception. He not only viewed education from an existential viewpoint, but established an extensive existential philosophy of education which corresponds to his "I-Thou" dialogic philosophy. Indeed, his unique educational existential philosophy may prove to be the intellectual ancestor and the ideological blue print of the authentic modern open school. The Heidelberg conference served as the platform for Buber's new educational ideology.

The Development of Creative Powers

The organizers of the Heidelberg Conference apparently assumed that the purpose of education is "the development of the creative powers in the child" and invited Buber to elaborate on this topic. However, as soon as Buber began his address, it became clear that he strongly differed with the educational philosophy of his hosts. He took issue with the position that the task of education is to develop the creative powers of the child and set out to develop his own educational theory.

In every hour, he explained, new human beings are born across the extent of our planet and our human race begins anew. These new-born human beings are already characterized and determined at birth, yet still determinable and open for further characterization. Each child, he proclaimed, is born with a given disposition of a world historical origin that is inherited from the riches of the whole human race, yet each child brings with him primal potential might, undeveloped newness, which are ready to be developed. The deeds of the new born children can illuminate the grey face of our creation or plunge it into deep darkness. What these children make of this universe depends upon their encounter with the earth into which they are born. It is the teacher who determines the nature of this encounter and therefore it is the teacher who holds great stakes in the decision-making process of the malleable child. The teacher knows the world in which the child lives and it is the teacher who serves as the selective sieve through which our life style reaches the child. Thus understood, education is defined as an encounter between the child and its world. The future of our civilization depends on this encounter and to a greater extent upon the teacher who directs this encounter. The teacher either rises up and assumes this task consciously, willingly and with responsibility and thus strengthens the light-spreading force in the heart of his pupils or loses his legitimacy as an educational motivator.

We learn from the above expose that from Buber's point of view the child is not creative, nor does he possess creative powers. Consequently, the liberation of these powers cannot be equated with education and their release is not an educational task.

Buber's views on man's "creativity" come to light when we reexamine his metaphysical position concerning Determinism and Indeterminism. The Determinists claim that man, like all earthly objects, is subject to absolute causality, and that his power of will is no more than a link in the causal chain of our world. The Indeterminist, on the other hand, claims that man, by virtue of his possession of the unique gift of free-will and self-determination, has permanent dominion over the world which is in itself passive, powerless and non-consequential. By virtue of his intellectual endowment he is continually engaged in the transformation of his world. So it is with the child. He is not a creator and indeed only part of creation. By virtue of his humanness he does not accept the world passively, but rather actively participates in its transformation. Here Buber concurs with the ancient Rabbis of Israel who taught that God has created the world but left it in an unfinished state so that man might serve as His partner and improve it towards greater perfection. This idea is reflected in the following passages:

Tineus Rufus asked Rabbi Akiba: "who makes more beautiful things, God or man?" Rabbi Akiba answered: "man makes more beautiful things." He showed him ears of grain and cakes and said, "the ears of grain are God's work, the cakes are man's. You see that man's works are more beautiful." Then he brought him raw flax and some finished linen garments of Beth Shean. He said to him "you see again that what man creates is more beautiful."[32] "Whatever was created by God during the six days of creation needs further improvement: for example, mustard needs sweetening, vetches need sweetening, wheat needs grinding."[33]

Indeed, man, the creature, who forms and transforms the creation cannot create, explained Buber, but he possesses tools which enable him to participate in the transformation of the world. Buber called these tools Instincts: The instinct of Origination and the Instinct of Communion.

Instinct of Origination

The Instinct of Origination is autonomous, spontaneous and non-derivatory from any other primal element such as "libido" or "will to power." It is a tool which brings man into active involvement in the progress of the human race. It constitutes an urge to make things, instead of merely existing purposelessly. Due to this instinct, the child is not a satisfied observer of happenings but one who desires to share actively in their production and to bring forth something which was not there before.[34] This instinct is of great significance to education and it is essential that the educator recognizes that it could serve as a viable tool in the process of education. This instinct is unique. It never becomes greed because it does not wish to possess, it only wishes to do. It grows only to passion but never to lust. It has no desire to invade the lives of others. It does not aim to snatch the world to itself, but to express itself to the world. It is a force which is directed outward. It creates and gives away to the world the object of its creation. It is a power within man which impresses itself on the material. When the movement is over, it has run its course in one direction, from the hearts' dream into the world, and its path is finished. As in the case of an artist,

33

a painter, or a sculptor, the originator gives away his product. At times he does not even know who is the recipient of his creation, and seldom learns whether the creation of his soul was favorably accepted by his anonymous recipient. He stands alone, always giving, never receiving. Consequently the originator is a solitary man, and "an education based only on the training of the instinct of origination would prepare a new human solitariness, which would be the most painful of all."[35] Following this theory, we deduce that the child's instinct of origination is not the core of education, nor does it represent the total task of education. The originative instinct left to itself does not lead nor can it lead to what is sharing in an understanding and to entering into mutuality with other people.

True, the instinct of origination is important in the process of education. Through this instinct we learn how to form things and how to put them together. We discover their origin and their structure. Yet, the instinct of origination cannot teach us the being of the world and the viaticum of life which are the heart and core of education.

Instinct of Communion

Real education, then, is not manifested through the instinct of origination. Real education is made possible through another instinct, one that "is longing for the world to become present to us as a person, which goes out to us as we to it, which chooses and recognizes us as we do it, which is confirmed in us as we in it."[36] It is the instinct which teaches us to see our fellow man and the world at large as a "Thou."

Education means growth and becoming, and this in-

stinct leads to growth and becoming. These developments are made possible only through interpersonal
relations, through encounter, not through solitude. Education is a total act of the total man through cooperation
and involvement with other people. This is not the function of the originative instinct. The instinct which does
teach us the saying of "Thou" and makes people relate
to each other as people is the Instinct of Communion.

Communion, authentic human relationship, is the kernel of education and its process is dialogue. Dialogue has
many faces and need not always be verbal. A child who
is lying with half closed eyes waiting for its mother to
speak to it is also conducting dialogue. Fortunately,
"many children need not wait, for they know that they
are unceasingly addressed in a dialogue which never
breaks off."[37] These children know that they are continu-
ously guarded by a mother who exists for them even
during the moments when she is not immediately and
physically present. It is the feeling of trust in the mother's availability which creates the most inward relationship. When the feeling of steady presence, actual or
potential, has been established, subterranean and endur-
ing mutuality has been assured. Putting it in Buber's
words: "only if someone grasps (the pupil's) hand not
as a 'creator' but as a fellow creature lost in the world,
to be his comrade or friend or lover beyond the arts,
does he have an awareness and a share of mutuality."[38]

Buber differentiates between three major forms of
dialogical experiences which he considered to be the
foundations of human interrelations. The first is the
experience of Awareness, the second is the experience of
Inclusion and the third is the experience of Friendship.

Dialogue of Awareness

Buber explained the dialogue of awareness as the case of two men feuding over a lingering dispute. Stubbornly both men hold on to their views and refuse to compromise their positions. Suddenly, and for no apparent reason, as by an invisible power, each becomes aware of the position of the other. Not that they agree with each other, but each of them suddenly sees the issue from the point of view of his opponent and each begins to understand his opponent's position. "What an illumination!"[39] True, even at this moment of illumination, the positions of the disputants have not altered and each still maintained his previous view, yet, a major change did occur. Each disputant has recognized the subjective position of his opponent's point of view. Each becomes aware what it is with the other as with himself. In Buber's opinion such perception of an opponent, even though he is still an opponent, is genuine communication and a true "I-Thou" relationship.

Kurzweil[40] pointed at an episode from the life of Buber which exemplifies this type of dialogue. At the approach of the First World War, distinguished personalities of many countries met to establish a supra-national authority, hoping to forestall hostilities. One of the participants raised the consideration that too many Jews had been nominated to the committee. Buber protested against the protest. In the course of the discussion, they came to speak of Jesus and Buber claimed that the Jews knew Jesus "from within." The clergyman stood up and so did Buber. They stared at each other and each examined the other's point of view. At a given instant each understood the other's position. Then the clergyman said: "It is gone" and in full view of the gathering they gave each other a kiss of brotherhood. They each became aware of one another's viewpoint and "the discussion of the situation between Jews and Christians had been transformed into a bond between the Christian and the Jew."[41]

Buber considered this type of dialogue, the dialogue of awareness, to be only partial and incomplete, related to man merely as a spiritual person and thus bound to leave out the full reality of his life and full being. This is a dialogue on the intellectual level only and is not a dialogue of the highest order.

Dialogue of Inclusion

A higher order dialogue which is the essence of the teacher-pupil relationship is the experience of inclusion. To more fully comprehend the important role of this type of dialogue in the process of education, one must bear in mind Buber's definitions of education and learning.

Learning, according to Buber, is continuous and coincidental. The whole environment, nature and society —the home, the street, the language, music, science— teaches human beings both by mere contact and indirect action. Genuine education, on the other hand, must be purposeful, deliberately willed, and understandingly executed by the teacher. In this process the teacher purposely and consciously selects the effective world for the child. This means that the teacher is given decisive effective powers to select for the pupil a world which is concentrated and manifested in him, the teacher. In this way the world becomes the true subject of the educational effect through the teacher.

All too often the teacher's selection of the effective world for the pupil is fraught with danger, because the teacher's will to educate may degenerate to arbitrariness and the realistic needs of his pupil may be subordinate to his own selfish vantage point. Yet, genuine education, where the teacher selects the effective world of his pupil, can be exercised without degenerating into self-willed unreasonableness. This is accomplished through the employment of the second type of dialogue: the experience of inclusion.

The experience of inclusion is the core of teacher-pupil relationship. In this experience the teacher must not only be cognizant of the effect of his action upon his pupil, but he must also view himself and his influence through his pupil's eyes. He must be aware how the environment and its events are viewed from "over-there," from the point of view of the pupil. Inclusion does not mean merely recognizing the child's individuality, or experiencing him as a spiritual person, or acknowledging him as a person. Inclusion means that the teacher "catches himself 'from over there,' and feels how it affects one, how it affects one, how it affects this other human being, (only then) does he recognize the real limit, baptize his self-will in reality and make it true will, and renew his paradoxical legitimacy."[42]

The experience of inclusion helps the teacher experience from that "over there" point of view of the pupil what the pupil accepts and what he rejects of his surrounding environment. Thus the teacher gains insight into the present needs of his pupil, realizing at the same time what is not needed. The teacher is now more adequately prepared to assist his pupils in their future growth.

Inclusion is, and must remain, one sided. If education is to take place, there cannot be a mutual relationship between the teacher and his pupil for according to Buber, when the pupil is able to throw himself across and experience from 'over there,' the educative relation would be burst asunder. Only the teacher may experience his pupil being educated, but the pupil must not experience the educating of his teacher. In the experience of inclusion, as we have noted, the teacher stands on both ends of the educational process, viewing his teaching from his own end and also from the point of view of the pupil. The pupil, however, views his education only from his own end. Should a mutual relationship arise, education can no longer take place, for now the teacher and his pupil will have entered into the third form of relationship, the relationship of friendship, and such a relationship robs the teacher of his strength to select the effective world of his pupil. Buber concluded that genuine education means "the selection of the effective world by a person and in him. The educator gathers in the constructive forces of the world. He distinguishes, rejects, and confirms in himself, in his self which is filled with the world. The constructive forces are eternally the same; they are the world bound up in community, turned to God. The educator educates himself to be their vehicle."[43]

Teaching and Deed

MARTIN BUBER, like his mentor Ahad Ha-Am, was a cultural Zionist. He could not perceive Israel as a mere political entity, another state among the states of the Middle East. He certainly recognized the need for the establishment of Israel as a place of refuge for any Jew in distress or for any Jew wishing to return to his ancient homeland, but to him this was not enough. For Buber the primary goal for the re-establishment of Israel as a state was to found a cultural and an intellectual center for the world-wide Jewish civilization. He viewed this center as the melting pot for the flowing of creative Jewish thoughts which would be generated the world over. It would serve as a sieve and a crucible in which the thoughts would be sifted and refined. By design and purpose it would serve as a store house for the age-old Jewish culture and as a birth place for a renewed spirit of the ancient prophets. From here, old, new and re-newed thoughts would be transmitted to the branches of Jewish civilization the world over. He viewed Israel and Jerusalem in the Biblical spirit which proclaimed that "out of Zion would come forth learning and the word of God from Jerusalem."

In the early thirties he watched with concern the rise of a pragmatic spirit within a segment of the Israeli community, a movement which placed great emphasis on deed, action, achievement, and performance. Buber feared that this pragmatic spirit, which gave preference to deed, would flourish at the expense of learning and scholarship, and that morals and values would be sacrificed for the sake of action. In the light of these concerns he gave expression to his views on the pedagogic problem of teaching versus deed. In his logical fashion he carefully analyzed the merits of traditional transmission of a culture from generation to generation, the need for change and recreation, the pitfalls which are inherent in teaching without deed, and the damaging consequences of action without a cognitive base. In light of the contemporary educational polemics this problem is just as relevant to educators today as it was when first expounded by Buber in 1934, at the Lehrhaus, in Frankfort-on-the-Main.

Cultural Transmission

Life means growth, and growth means propagation and regeneration, theorized Buber. This is true not only in the biological realm but also in the cultural and in the intellectual domain. Among humans, biological propagation and propagation of values exist side by side. If a civilization is to survive, its ideals and culture must be transmitted uninterruptedly from generation to generation, just as organic life is transmitted uninterruptedly from parents to children in order to guarantee the survival of that community. The agent for the cultural transmission is the teacher who, through the educational process, links generations one to another.

In Judaism, stated Buber, biological propagation and the propagation of the spirit are organically bound.

41

Israel is a people only by virtue of its cultural commitment. Its physical and spiritual characteristics are in-
separably intertwined. With this in mind the talmudic
sages stated that "he who teaches the tradition to his
fellow man is regarded as though he had formed and
made him, and brought him into the world."[44] In the
culture of ancient Israel the transmission of knowledge
was compared not only with the parental act of giving
birth to a child, but was set on a par with the divine
work of God himself. The sages claimed that the teacher
who "brings forth the precious out of the vile" in the
soul of a pupil offers him a second birth.[45] Even today
the cultural and the intellectual life of Israel is not a
superstructure, but a merger of its spiritual and physical
life which is the major purpose for its existence. In ancient Israel the propagation of values assumed the major
purpose of its life.

Cultural Change

Nevertheless, spiritual and physical life are not complete and inflexible entities which are simply transmitted
from generation to generation. Mere transmission of a
culture breeds stagnation and fails to induce intellectual
propagation. The values which are conveyed from a
host must take on new form in its recipient. They do not
represent the sum total of the heritage, they're only a
sperm which must grow and develop into a new, unique,
and independent organism, albeit, rooted in a fertile and
life-generating past. A people, as a living organism, must
be founded on its inherited tradition, but at the same
time must reconstruct and reshape its old tradition to
meet with the vital needs of its contemporary society.

42

The past must be ingrained within the present, yet the present in its refabrication and reevaluation must also germinate a new future. The task of the older generation is to teach, awaken and shape the younger generation, "then the holy spark leaps across the gap." The older generation encounters the young with mutual and radical interactions bringing forth changes in values, which is in truth a blend of the old and the new.

Learning Without Deed

Buber held that teaching is inseparable from deed; learning is useless without living; and the amassing of knowledge is not education. Teaching must be reflected in dynamic life experiences or it is not worthy of its name. Learning must not exist for its own sake; it must lead to deeds. Buber was quick to differentiate between the Greek concept SOPHIA and the Biblical Hebrew concept HOKHMAH. SOPHIA connotes knowledge for its own sake while HOKHMAH refers to the unity of teaching and life. While the Socratic man believed that all virtue is cognition, the Mosaic man insisted on the merger of learning and deed. Cognition is not enough because learning does not necessarily lead to perfor-mance. The Talmudic sages ruled that "one who studies with a different intent than act, it would have been more fitting for him never to have been created."[46] It also stated: "he whose deeds exceed his wisdom, his wisdom shall endure; but he whose wisdom exceeds his deeds, his wisdom shall not endure." In the final analysis, what counts most is not man's thoroughness of knowledge, keenness of thought or spiritual possession but the trans-lation of learning into deed.[47]

43

Deeds Without Learning

Teaching without deed, decided Buber, is irreconcilable, but in 1934 he realized, as contemporary humanists realize today, that the danger to education lies at the other end of the spectrum. He was aware that he lived in an era in which deeds asserted their superiority over learning. "The present generation," complained Buber, "universally believes more and more unreservedly that it can get along without the teachings and rely on a mode of action which—in its own opinion—is correct."[48] He conceded that the conduct of life without learning could lead to achievement. But achievement for what? The goals and purposes of a society, its aspirations and yearnings, must be transmitted through genuine teaching, and only then could these values be translated into action. Just as teaching can not stand apart from doing, so doing cannot be independent of teaching. A culture cannot continue uninterruptedly if its teaching is aborted. A civilization cannot be perpetuated on its biological substance alone. Nor will a land and a language by themselves maintain the civilization. Without the fiery breath of teaching a civilization cannot ward off decay. Only teaching links generations and maintains a culture.[49]

The students of Rabbi Akiba once asked: "What is greater, teachings or deeds?" Rabbi Akiba answered: "The teachings are greater!" and the students agreed saying: "The teachings are greater, for the teachings beget the deed."[50] Deeds are important, but it is teaching which gives direction and purpose to the actions in our lives.[51]

The Education of Character

BUBER RATED THE EDUCATION of character as the supreme goal of the educational endeavor. He rendered character education so important that he devoted to it a special monograph and declared emphatically that "education worthy of the name is essentially education of character." He explained that character education is global and all encompassing. It does not relate to any single function of the pupil but is concerned with the pupil as a total human being, both with his present actuality, as he now appears before us, and with all his possibilities, that which he can become.

He carefully differentiated between two commonly interchangeable words: personality and character. Personality, he explained, signifies what a person already is, what he has already become. It is that into which man has already developed both physically and spiritually. Thus, personality is a completion, a given. Being a completion, the personality of a pupil remains essentially outside the teacher's influence. The teacher may cultivate and enhance it, but the major energies in education must be directed at something more essential: at character education.

While personality is completion, character is a task. It is a leap to what lies ahead. It is the link between a particular individual personality and the consequence of

45

his actions and attitudes. The major aim of the genuine education must always be character education.

In order to understand Buber's educational theory concerning character development it is important to first understand his distinct definition of the term "education." In the American culture, the word "education" has been used to encompass the entire range of the teaching-learning process. Not so in the German language, Buber's native tongue. The German language draws a clear distinction between two clearly defined educational processes: "erziehung" and "bildung." "Erziehung" connotes instruction, the learning of a skill, a trade, or a profession, while "bildung" refers primarily to character education. American educators do not deem it necessary to distinguish between those two aspects, they include both courses in the term "education." Martin Buber, however, drew a clear distinction between "erziehung" and "bildung," between instruction, per se, and character education. "Instruction" according to Buber is relatively a simple task. One can give instruction in a subject like trigonometry and almost assure relative success in achievement. One can teach with success the idea of quadratic equation or the finding of an unknown in algebra. One can teach how to mix elements in chemistry and produce a new compound, but one cannot give instruction in ethics and expect transformation into character building substance. One may instruct a pupil that envy is despicable and that lying destroys life but the result will be no more than the transmission of information, and little will materialize in character development. Buber related a personal anecdote when he once tried to give instruction on honesty: "the worst habitual liar of the class produces a brilliant essay on the destructive

46

power of lying."[52] He confessed that he made a fatal mistake of giving instruction in ethics. What he said was accepted as current coin of knowledge, but nothing of it was transformed in character-building substance.

Character education is not an easy task, it is a formidable undertaking with fundamental limitations. In the ordinary educative process everything impresses and molds the pupil, and the shaping occurs without intention and without selection. Character education, however, is not coincidental. It is intentional, purposeful, and selective. Here the educator selects deliberately, by his will and by his consciousness, from his bank of knowledge and experience, what he considers to be right and what ideals should be pursued. It is this willful selection which makes for character education, but it is also this willful selection which brings about the resistance of the pupil.

We must not over-estimate the effectiveness of the educator, even at his best, in the developing of character. Conventional methods employed in instruction will disintegrate when employed in character education. Students generally wish to acquire knowledge and skills making the teacher's instructional task relatively easy, but they oppose external imposition of aims and goals on their lives. They resent superficial definitions of what is "good" and "evil," and rebel when one dictates to them, as though it were some long established truth, on the virtuous and the bane.

How does one communicate what is "right" and what "should be" to his pupils?

Character education cannot be achieved by giving instruction in ethics, nor through pedagogic gimmickry, nor by subterfuge. Even when the pupil misses the hidden motives of his teacher, it still has its negative effects on the educative process because character education can be achieved only by the directness and openness of the teacher. "Only in his whole being, in all his spontaneity can the educator truly affect the whole being of his pupil."[53] Subterfuge and gimmickry deprive the teacher himself of the directness which is his strength.

The teacher's only access to the totality of his pupil is to win his confidence. Only when the student's confidence has been won, his resistance against being educated gives way to a singular happening: he accepts his teacher as a person and begins to trust him. He feels that his teacher accepts him before desiring to influence him, and thus the pupil reaches the first step towards the education of his character: he learns to ask, the teacher answers, and a process of dialogue begins between them. In this process the teacher must not dictate what is good and what is evil, but must only answer concrete questions on what is right and what is wrong in a given situation. This process of dialogue, which functions only in an atmosphere of trust without any deliberate or politic intention, provides the environment for character education.

It is not necessarily implied that a pupil who enjoys the confidence of his teacher need always accept his teacher's views, nor does it indicate unconditional agreement. What we see is a breakthrough, a beginning of dialogue, the opening of a direct relationship. The teacher's only gain in this relationship is an opportunity to conduct a real battle for truth. If the teacher wins, he must stand ready to comfort his pupil with a word of love and help him endure the defeat. On the other hand, if he cannot conquer his pupil, the teacher must not permit either of them to degenerate into a contest of wills, nor can he allow the line of communication to be broken. The dialogue must never cease for it is in itself educative. Dialogue means that the dividing walls come tumbling down and the trusting pupil opens up for an interactive human process. In the final analysis "it is not the educational intentions but . . . the meeting which is educationally fruitful."[54]

When confidence is gained the road to the ultimate goal of education has been opened and the teacher is ready to foster and develop "the great character." Once we determine the significance and scope of "the great character" the difficulties confronting the teacher in pursuing character education are manifold. How does the teacher penetrate these difficulties? Buber understood the significance of these problems and set out to examine critically the concept of character itself.

To clarify his own concept of "character," he introduced definitions of his contemporaries with whom he took issue; one of Kerschensteiner who defined character as a "system of maxims" and that of Dewey to whom character was a "system of habits." According to Kerschensteiner's definition, character is "fundamentally nothing but voluntary obedience to the maxims which have been molded in the individual by experience, teaching, and self-reflection, whether they have been adopted and then completely assimilated or have originated in the consciousness through self-legislation."[55] This voluntary obedience is a form of self control which was instilled in the pupil through love or fear and was eventually turned into the habit of self-conquest. The process is that of outer obedience which consequently is transformed into inner obedience. This inner obedience creates the "real ethical character" which Kerschensteiner defined as "a special attitude, and one which in action gives the preference before all others to absolute values." Buber assumed that by absolute values Kerschensteiner had related to universal values and norms, the existence of which the person concerned recognizes and acknowledges. Unfortunately, lamented Buber, in our age, values and norms do not relate to a higher order than man which governs the whole of mankind, but to expressions of life of a specific group which translates its own needs into the language of objective claims, until the group itself is raised to an absolute value, and frequently into the only value.[56]

This problem constitutes a conflict between a world which for several millenia has believed in a truth superior to man, and our present age which believes it no longer. Today, hosts of people have sunk into the slavery of collectives, and each collective is the supreme authority of its own slaves. Such fragmentation of our civilization presents the existence of any universal sovereignty in idea, faith, or spirit. Such a situation denies, as well, the definition of character as a system of maxims which gives preference to absolute values in a universal sense.

Buber also took issue with John Dewey who defined character as "the interpenetration of habits." Dewey reasoned that without "the continued operation of all habits in every act" there would be no unified character, but only "a juxtaposition of disconnected reactions to separated situations." Buber argues that modern education is powerless precisely because it defines character as self-control by means of the accumulation of maxims or as a system of interpenetrating habits. "Not that the educators could dispense with employing useful maxims or furthering good habits, but in moments that come perhaps only seldom, a feeling of blessed achievement links him to the explorer, the inventor, the artist, a feeling of sharing in the revelations of what is hidden. In such moments he finds himself in a sphere very different from that of maxims and habits. Only on this highest plane of his activity can he fix his real goal, the real concept of character which is his concern, even though he might not often reach it."[57]

The task of the educator cannot consist of educating great characters. There is no process which could assure such a product. The educator can only introduce discipline and order, and hope that this discipline and order will become more and more inward and autonomous.[58] He cannot contrive a formula which will create the great character, yet, his real goal, which will influence all his work, remains the great character.

What is the great character which Buber is advocating?

Buber is an existentialist who believes in the uniqueness of each person and the right of each person to his particular uniqueness. The great character is neither a system of maxims nor a system of habits, nor does he follow predetermined maxims and habits. Each person reacts individually in accordance with the singularities of every situation which challenges him. True, there are similarities in circumstance and one can draw maxims and habits which are common to different occasions, yet, despite the similarities, each situation is different and notable. Each requires a distinctive reaction which cannot be prepared beforehand. It exacts nothing of what is past. "It demands presence, responsibility. A great character is one who by his actions and attitudes satisfies the claim of situations out of deep readiness to respond with his whole life, and in such a way that the sum of his actions and attitudes expresses at the same time the unity of his being and his willingness to accept responsibility."[59]

Buber agrees that the great character is not beyond the acceptance of norms. No responsible person places himself above norms, but norms must never be turned into maxims and habits. Any command that the great character takes to himself remains latent substance until it reveals itself to him in a concrete way. Even the most universal norm must not be turned into a maxim nor a habit, but is recognized by the pupil only in a very special situation. In such a special situation the norm comes forth as an inner command, a command which emerges not because it is an outcome of a maxim or a habit, but his own self commands him of what is right and what should be.[60]

Where does the modern educator begin with the process of character education?

Buber insisted that it is the responsibility of each person to determine for himself the choice of his own destiny. He believed that the major task of education is to awaken in the pupils the desire to assume responsibility for their actions. He was highly critical of our modern day young people who are absorbed by their political and social collectives and as a result have lost their personal responsibility for life and the world. These young people are blindly devoted to their collective only because of their fear to be left alone to their own resources and to rely on themselves. They do not realize that their blind devotion to their collective is no more than an escape from responsibility which they fear to face. They fear responsibility because in our age they no longer receive directions from universal values which are of a higher order than man and are common to all mankind. They do not realize that "he who no longer, with his whole being, decides what he does or does not, and assumes responsibility for it, becomes sterile in soul. And a sterile soul soon ceases to be a soul."[61]

This is where the educator can begin. He can awaken in his pupil the need for clarity of consciousness, the force of desire, and particularly the courage to shoulder life again. He can make his pupil aware of the great character as a model who faces all challenges and accepts responsibility for every essential he encounters. In this process the pupil will learn that discipline and order are starting points toward self-responsibility. This model of the great character will exemplify to the pupil the concept of unity of being which must precede man's actions and attitudes. "This does not mean a static unity of the uniform, but the great dynamic unity of the multiform in which multiformity is formed into a unity of character."[62] The task of the educator is to foster and develop a longing for personal unity which is the cornerstone for the unity of mankind, for only "genuine education of character is genuine education for community." In the final analysis, "the educator who helps to bring man back to his own unity will help to put him again face to face with God."[63]

The Education of Adults

The Problem

AT THE TURN OF THE CENTURY, after two thousand years of exile, the Jewish people began their return to their ancient native land. This return was designed with the aim of establishing an independent creative homeland for a stateless people. The early idealistic settlers realized a great measure of success in their venture to develop not only a homeland but a new type of person, a pioneer, an idealist, a prototype for their emerging society. The purpose of that new society was "to amalgamate the pioneers into a new unity, a unity with a central core, which would overcome the distances of being and the distances of souls between the communities, that would assure future unity."[64] This effort was soon aborted by the Nazi holocaust. The catastrophic wave of destruction and annihilation during World War II brought about global disaster which was particularly devasting to the Jewish people whose toll amounted to six million dead—one third of its world population.

The termination of World War II and the creation of the state of Israel brought about an unprecedented wave of immigrants into that country. They came from many lands and comprised an extremely diversified multitude. They differed in their cultures, languages, and

54

ways of life, and constituted a tapestry of culturally and materially deprived individuals and societies. The immediate need was to establish a social, economic, and cultural base which could encompass the established life-types of those who settled in the land prior to World War II together with the expanse of the new sub-cultures. Thus, the primary need was for an organic plan, aimed toward the amalgamation of all the diversifications into some form of cohesiveness, whose purpose it would be to remove the existing barriers and promote a social and national unity based on a common economic and cultural foundation. Many of the new immigrants lacked even a proper elementary schooling. Not that they were illiterate, but they had no working knowledge of the language, the culture, and the democratic life-style of their new society. To educate hundreds of thousands of adult immigrants so that they may become mature enough to participate fully in the life of a democratic state became the second felt need.[65]

The mass immigration made the pre-World War II evolutionary plan inoperative. There was "no time to wait for the necessities of communal life to iron out imbalanced inequalities in a span of several generations,"[66] and the conventional process of educating elementary and secondary school children toward the realization of these aims was deemed inexpeditious. The task was urgent and could not wait another generation.

Martin Buber, called to draft a solution to this pressing problem, believed that a viable and dynamic adult education program was the only conceivable vehicle and that the teacher of adults was its chief agent. He believed, however, that ordinary teachers would not qualify as teachers of adults. He argued that "the graduates of teachers' training seminaries are usually able to deal well with children, while the university and other institutions of higher learning, as a rule, turn out teachers who are specialists in certain subjects. None of them therefore are suitably prepared for the task of adult education."[67] Thus in 1949 Buber founded the Teachers' Institute for the Education of Adults and became its chief architect. He conceived the aims and purposes of his school and its process of learning, defined the nature and qualifications of its teachers, and designed an educational model befitting his existential-universal concepts.

The Purpose

Buber, unlike his contemporaries, could not accept nationalism and national unity as the major aims of his new society. These could not serve as a meaningful and dynamic purpose in a world of human affliction, division, intrigue, confusion and hopelessness, Moreover, he could not see two thousand years of yearning and suffering culminate in the mere formation of another people among the peoples of the world and the creation of another singular nation among the world's nations. He was determined that the new emerging society required an extraordinary aim and purpose, a raison d'être.

Buber perceived the mass immigration and the physical formation of the new society in Israel as an exceptional opportunity to bring his existential-universal-humanistic philosophy into fruition. World War II challenged old dogmas, destroyed old absolutes, and shattered old ways of life. The established philosophies did not hold true in the light of the new reality. Man's faith in external omnipotent forces and in supernatural benevolence had been crushed in the European gas chambers; scientific knowledge proved to be instrumental—a tool merely for living and little else, and the hopes which man placed on the new social order were rendered sterile and did not rescue him in his hour of peril. Man remained alone, searching for salvation within himself and from himself.

Buber believed that the solution to man's problems did not rest in more knowledge, nor in more skills, not even in the enrichment of man's mind. He believed that the future of mankind lay in eternal-universal values, the only values which could forge a diversity of individuals into a cohesive entity, and that education worthy of its name must be directed toward the fostering of a continuous desire for these values. Such values require a suitable base, a humanistic and global foundation which would serve as a common denominator and reach out beyond the narrow confines of subcultures. He looked for values which would transcend the boundaries of political parties or ethnic collectives, to unite the many segments of his community.[68]

Addressing himself to the burning issue at hand—the re-establishment of Israel as a viable, purposeful society—Buber proclaimed that "there is no future for Israel as a people without a yearning desire to return to the eternal values; without such a yearning desire even the unification of the people of Israel in its land cannot materialize. Only a yearning desire to return (to eternal values) will unite the exiles. Consequently, the education of the immigrants, more so the education of adults in an era of mass immigration, must be aimed at a desire to return to eternal values."[69]

The teaching of values does not negate nor diminish the teaching of subject matter, but the teaching of subject matter, according to Buber, becomes a vehicle toward the attainment of an educational goal. He claimed that subject matter such as Hebrew, Bible history and geography should not be taught merely to transmit more knowledge. "The Hebrew language needs to be taught not only for its own sake but as a carrier of our share in the eternal values. The Bible needs to be taught not only as a par excellence possession of our national culture, but also as the commitment of the people of Israel to the world of eternal values. Similarly it is not sufficient to explore the path of this nation in the span of time through the study of history, but obligatory to comprehend the essence and the core of historic events which serve witness that this nation did not proclaim and promote the values of righteousness and peace out of weakness, but because of loyalty in what it believed. Even the geography of the land needs to be taught in the spirit of the promise which this land holds for all mankind. In a word, the student needs to learn the reality of life, but his eyes and heart must be opened to see that his reality must be a means to the truth of the spirit and its path in the world."[70]

Buber's most cherished values were the prophetic values. He proposed that the greatest national treasure of Israel is its prophetic concepts and insisted that nationalism is a divisive and isolationistic element which is alien to the spirit and essence of Israel. He insisted that only the prophetic universal and eternal values could serve as the core of modern Israel and as the catalyst for its spiritual rejuvenation, and that Israel must entwine its prophetic heritage with the spirit of mankind toward a struggle for eternal values—a struggle which will return to man the trust in the meaningful purpose of world and of life."[71]

The School

"The real struggle," Buber said one day, "is not between East and West, or capitalism and communism, but between education and propaganda. Education means teaching people to see the reality around them and to understand it for themselves. Propaganda is exactly the opposite. It tells the people, 'You will think like this, as we want you to think!'

"Education lifts the people up. It opens their hearts and develops their minds, so that they can discover the truth and make it their own. Propaganda, on the other hand, closes their hearts and stunts their minds. It compels them to accept dogmas without asking themselves, 'Is this true or not?'

"The trouble is that this is not only a conflict of ideology. It is a conflict of tempo. The tempo of propaganda is feverish, nervous. It is the pace of television and the radio. It is the pace of newspaper headlines; the cry of the vendor in the street."[72]

Buber was greatly concerned with the role of propaganda in our modern society and observed with alarm the forces which desired to impose their authority and control on their fellow man. In 1949 he seized the opportunity to combat propaganda when he was invited to establish the Teachers' Institute for the Education of Adults. He had no desire to establish just another teacher's institute, but saw in the new institute a unique opportunity to field test and to implement his theory of education for a free and humanistic society which is devoid of propaganda and imposition. He embraced with

59

delight the humanistic theories of the 19th century philosophers Bolzano and Grundtvig which he readily incorporated in his essay "Adult Education." This essay served as a blue print and a plan for action for his teacher's institute.

The purpose of a teachers' institute for adults, he concurred with Bolzano, is to spread truth for the good of the public. Toward this goal youth must be educated diligently in the art of correct thinking so that they could recognize the decadent concepts which surround them and would not be led astray by those who aim to misguide them. They must be taught to investigate wisely and critically what is true and deserves their trust. Youth, he explained, is a critical stage in the human life. As children they have been provided in elementary and secondary school with abundant information, but as young adults they must learn something they were unable to learn before. They must learn how to critically analyze their acquired knowledge and independently form their own opinions. Their decisions must be based on the reality of their present life and their daily encounters.

To this point Buber agreed with all other existentialists, but now their roads part. The exclusive concern of the existentialists with the individual caused them to neglect the society, while Buber's concern was not only with the freedom of man, but with the free man within the context of his free society.

He was involved not only with man but also with mankind. He joined forces with the Danish scholar Grundtvig who insisted that independent, critical and analytical thinkers must not remain in isolation, but are duty bound to serve in the forefront toward the establishment of a permanent and highly cultured society. Only the assemblage of critical observers and free de-cision makers can bring about such a social life-style.

Both Buber and Grundtvig proposed that the curricu-lum of a teachers' institute for adults must be founded on two elements: first, it must be based on the historical, traditional, ethnic, and even mythological foundations of the people; second, it must be closely related to the needs of the contemporary society. For them, the means to achieve these goals is by dialogue. Through dialogue both the teacher and the pupil observe and analyze the re-alities of life and together contribute from their stores of knowledge and experience to the improvement and progress of their society. In such a dialogue clear minds and dynamic souls interact. These interactions refine the thoughts and bring about unprecedented learning. The questions of the student about the unknown and the unclear, the answers of the teacher, and the intellectual intercourse among the students themselves constitute the dialogical principle of education.[73] This is a process of interpersonal, open and free interaction which brings the teacher and the student together. It provides for en-counter and mutuality, and constitutes the foundation for genuine education.

Like Grundtvig, Buber believed that a teachers' insti-tute for adults must be based on science and research but must never become an adjunct to science. It must maintain its spiritual and intellectual strength to meet with the immediate needs of the hour and with the needs of life. By "needs of life" and "needs of the hour" he referred to the service which should be provided to a given people at a given historical hour to overcome its problems.[74]

As did Grundtvig, Buber realized that a teachers' institute for adults must be field centered. While other disciplines could probably be learned through lectures and exercises, teacher education can be made possible only through direct field experiences. The pupils must be removed from their ordinary occupations for months or even years and be turned into a work-study community which is taught directly through real life experiences.[75]

Buber lived through a period when education was perplexed. It was perplexed because the twentieth century brought in its wake giant changes in our sociological structure, technological patterns, occupational practices and primarily in our philosophic grasp of the concept of man and society. While major stride has been made in many of man's endeavors, education was caught straggling behind, perennially attempting to catch up with a run-away civilization. In this catch-up race educators have been attempting to superimpose on education some technological and structural innovations which were borrowed from industry, and proposed to reform education through refined teaching methods, improved skills and advanced technology. Toward this end, contemporary educators have been expending much energy and resources on the content of education and on teaching strategies. As in industry, educators specified behavioral objectives and educational outcomes. They set up criteria-referenced goals and directed their pupils to obtain given prescribed knowledge, skills and behaviors.

That Buber rejected this approach to learning is obvious from the story which he told about Christian Cold, an educator in the Danish adult education movement. Once a young farmer came to Cold and complained that he listened diligently to his master's lectures but occasionally forgot their content. Said Cold: "you need not worry about that. Just observe your own work in the field. When you place drainage pipes in the ground, you carefully mark their location so that you could relocate them when you need them again. Not so when you sow corn. When you sow corn, you do not mark their spots because they grow and sprout in their proper season on their own accord. So it is with you. What you have learned in leisure will surface just when you will need it."

As a pedagogue true to the name, Buber differentiated between instruction and education. Instruction aims to engrave in the memory of the pupil the largest amount of information in all the areas of knowledge, and ascertain that this knowledge is retrievable upon command. Genuine education, on the other hand, aspires to educate the pupil so that his acquired knowledge becomes an organic part of his whole life. With little luck the knowledge which the genuine educator implants in the pupil grows and bears fruit effortlessly, just like the corn which grows and sprouts effortlessly out of the ground. In order to achieve this goal, adult education must be directed not only to man's mind but to the totality of man. It needs to teach the future teacher "to think not only with his brain but with his entire spiritual and even his physical entity, with all his limbs and all his senses." In short, the purpose of the teachers' institute is to foster a renewed organic character of the pupil's spirit.[76]

Buber maintained that the Teachers' Institute for Adult Education is not a continuation of the elementary and secondary school educational establishments. It does not aim to provide its students with additional information, nor does it propose to compete with the university whose purpose it is to prepare pupils for research or for the activity of the mind in given disciplines. The Teachers' Institute strives to educate its pupils to meet the needs of their contemporary society. Of course, the university, too, is interested in this objective, but only to a limited degree. The university, he explained, teaches and indirectly educates, while the Teachers' Institute educates its pupils through teaching; it educates its pupils to become good citizens of independent thoughts."[77]

But can we educate adults?

Buber held that our society had convinced itself that its main educational target is its children, and expended most of its educational energies and resources on the young. But this is wrong, he claimed. He insisted that "education worthy of the name is essentially education of character," and that character education must be an ongoing process for life. Buber knew that it is possible, even though difficult, to modify the character of children but he also knew that to educate adults is arduous and problematic. Children and youth are in a developmental stage and are still amenable to influence and change, but the character of the adult is essentially fixed. The adult has established opinions and a life-style not easily subject to change. Regrettably these views and life-styles are frequently not his own inner creation but those which he accepted from his social and political collective. The adult assumes that his potentiality has matured, that he has already been educated, and that his character has already been formed. What the adult seeks is not education but more knowledge and more information. Ironically, what the adult needs most in many cases, is precisely what he does not want-character education. He needs character education because during adolescence

64

the character of youth is frequently shaped hastily and haphazardly, and their self-confidence to handle the realities of life is often false. The task of adult education is to weaken and uproot this false self-confidence in absolutes and unfounded truisms. Adult education must arouse in the pupil the desire for independent research for truth and the readiness and willingness to serve the society in which he lives.

The Teacher of Adults

Buber considered the teacher to be the prime factor in the educational enterprise. He held him in high regard and accorded him a noble position on the social and professional scale. He gave special attention to the teacher of adults and carefully defined his educational role and responsibilities. He believed that teachers of adults must possess unique qualities and skills not ordinarily found in teachers of children and youth, and thus require special training to achieve the competency demanded of their vocation. He was not satisfied with the teachers whose ordinary orbit was elementary or secondary education and were also engaged in adult education as an adjunct to their main occupation. He proclaimed that adult education "is not a secondary occupation to be resorted to in default of anything better, but a calling of primary importance which makes upon those who follow it no fewer demands than any other calling. Indeed, it is more exacting than other professions, for it claims the person's entire being"[78] and complete devotion to education. Thus it is incumbent upon the nation, the state and the national institutions to confer upon the teacher and his occupation proper recognition and support, so that education might become a highly respected occupation.

Buber viewed the educator of adults as the kernel of his program. He maintained that it is not teaching that educates but the teacher. Like Socrates, a good teacher does not exert his influence by what he teaches but through his teaching personality. "It is the good teacher who educates with his words and with his silence; during the teaching hours and during recess; in a casual conversation; by his mere being—as long as his presence is really there. He educates through contact, a contact between the teacher and his pupils."[79] Buber held that education of adults differs from any other profession. While other professions demand from the professional quality knowledge and performance, adult education demands not only mastery of subject matter and proficiency in skills, but also intimate knowledge of the pupil and personal contact with him. Intellectual and spiritual intercourse is the root and basis of adult education for the spark of education is ignited only when the teacher establishes contact between his personality and the personality of the pupil. Unlike training, genuine education does not maintain one way transmission, from the teacher to the student, but a process of reciprocity and interchange between the mature mind of the teacher and the formative mind of the pupil. In this reciprocal process both the teacher and the pupil act as partners, both communicate without restraint and both give and take in a genuine dialogue.

Buber insisted that contact and dialogue in the teaching process of adults must never deteriorate into meaningless chatter. The teaching of adults must be purposeful and responsible and must be based on clear and precise concepts. He was fond of the story about a ruler in ancient China who wished to invite Confucius to head the government. When a student asked Confucius what his first reforms would be, he answered: "concept clarification." He considered clear concepts to be of prime importance because "whenever concepts are incorrect, the words used are not apt: and whenever words are not apt, actions are not performed . . . therefore, anyone seeking to train men to understand the task for teachers of people must in the first place inculcate in them a sense of responsibility with regard to concepts and speech."[80] Thus the teacher of adults needs to clarify concepts, particularly in the realm of the humanities and the social sciences, which deal with the social, cultural and political realities of life.

He asserted that a philosophy of education must not be an abstract theory but is to serve as a blueprint for daily living. He advised the teachers of adults to design their entire adult education curriculum to meet the mundane problems of their pupils, and "whatever is not connected, either directly or indirectly, with the reality of our life should have no place in their curriculum."[81]

Buber declared that teachers, and particularly teachers of adults, must not dictate to their pupils. Students must be permitted to reach their own conclusions. The "business of the teacher is to answer a concrete question, to answer what is right and wrong in a given situation. . . . By trying to answer it to the best of (his) knowledge and conscience (he) helps it to become a character that actively overcomes contradictions."[82]

67

The Education of Youth

BUBER WAS A DEDICATED TEACHER who remained stead-fast to his convictions. He held himself responsible to educate youth not by imposing self-evident righteous formulae and absolute answers but through reasoning and directing, then leaving the decisions to the pupils themselves. He treated his pupils as partners in the educational enterprise and gave them credit when credit was due, yet taking issue with them when he believed them wrong. He blamed the adult leadership for its hypocrisy concerning truth, responsibility, faith and spirit, but neither did he spare youth for relegating its responsibilities and seeking escape in biased prejudices. With forthright honesty he stood before his students to reason and argue his case concerning their biases and responsibilities. Buber maintained that "young people are apt to think that prejudices are something peculiar to age, and that they themselves are unbiased and free from all prejudice." But this is not so. To be prejudiced means to pass judgement prior to experience, and of this, youth is guilty. Young people too often take sides on issues not on the basis of experience, making decisions hurriedly on the basis of passion and emotion. They resist comparing judgement because they fear contest and contradiction. They seek out only those experiences which tend to confirm their position.

Buber, the conscientious and outspoken teacher, cautioned youth on the dangers of prejudice. It is this trait, he told them, that boxes man in and keeps him from accepting the new and the untried. He taught youth that an open mind was their most precious human possession. He urged them to "remain open to the whole world, see what there is to see, experience what experience offers, and include all of experience in the effectuation of whatever cause one has decided for. Though constantly changing, our stand will yet remain true to itself, but deepened by an insight which grows more and more true to reality."[83] Prejudices, he believed, are not necessarily bad. Some strengthen the individual and still leave him with an open mind. He held that youth must take a firm position, yet be able to stand free and unbiased to face the realities of life.

Of the many biases of youth, Buber was particularly concerned with their prejudice against history. He claimed that young people assume that the world begins with them. They reject the effects of past history and the forces which produced the present generation and thus prevent the stream of tradition from affecting their lives. True, every new generation must have faith in itself and must blaze its own path of life, but at the same time it must not divert itself from its great inheritance of eternal values. While young people produce their own new ring in the chain of history, they must link it to their great heritage which is the product of past generations. Youth must have the essential knowledge that the generations which produced them are within them, and whatever new thing they accomplished draws its real significance from that fact.

The prejudice of youth against the spirit was another

of Buber's concerns. "I am deeply distressed" he said "to find a great number of our young people sharing a prejudice against spirituality—even though I quite understand how this came about. It is not difficult to comprehend why many now guard themselves against having faith or confidence in the spirit. For during the past decades the race of man has not, by and large, fared well at the hands of the spirit. For the spirit was not simply silent; it spoke falsely at junctures when it should have had an important voice in history, when it should have told the truth about what was being done or not being done to those who were making or seemed to be making history. On frequent occasions the spirit consented to be a tool when it should have acted on its own in the capacity of judge and censor. Then again, it has repeatedly retired to a magnificent isolated kingdom of its own, poised high above the world in the realm of circling ideas."[84]

Buber reasoned that the negative actions which are attributed to the spirit are not genuine. They were performed by counter-faith spirit which managed to deceive a great many people. Youth, too, was deceived. Nevertheless, it must not stop believing in the power of the great spirit, for if it does it will destroy the foundations of our existence and even our right to exist. Youth must capture the genuine spirit, and if this spirit cannot be readily found, youth must set forth to search for it and renew its vitality.

But not only the spirit of man wronged our youth. The traditional concepts of our adult community, the truth which it held, its sense of responsibility, its sense of spontaneity, its sense of faith—all failed youth. None exemplified what they explicated. Little wonder that youth felt perplexed.

Buber set out to reason with youth on another bias: their prejudice against truth. He believed that youth misunderstood the concept of truth. He observed with concern the growing number of young people who converted to the erroneous idea that truth is relative and subject to the biased interpretation of each individual without an examination of its validity. He, of course, rejected the idea of one general absolute truth. He himself relentlessly expounded his humanistic and existential belief that each person is endowed with the inalienable freedom to think, to know, and to express himself freely on the basis of his own particular being. But he voiced his protest against those youth who in a moment of crisis sought escape into the darkness of unconditional truth. He was also perturbed by those youth who, on the force of the theory that truth is relative, labeled "truth" anything which served their selfish purposes rather than set up an hypothesis, a deepening search for truth to validate their findings. He taught youth that there is no truth that "we can pick up and put in our pocket. But the individual can have a honest and uncompromising attitude toward the truth and hold and uphold it all his life." He taught that youth must try to translate its relationship to truth into the reality of its own life and stand ready to answer for it.[85]

Another subject which concerned Buber, the educator, was the misconception of youth on individual freedom and personal responsibility. He believed that youth was directed against such responsibility and considered it the obligation of educators to attempt to rectify this prejudice.

He concurred with the proclamation of Henry David Thoreau who said in Walden: "There will never be a really free and enlightened state until the state comes to recognize the individual as a higher and independent power, from which all of its power and authority are derived." Like Thoreau he was concerned with bureau-cratic superstratum and the spirit of collectivism which threatens to engulf the individual man.[86] Like Kierke-gaard he protested against any exaltation of society at the price of submerging the individual. Buber disagreed, however, with Kierkegaard who called for an aristocratic anarchy which would give free reign to the individual. Instead Buber taught youth "to recognize the insight that true community among men cannot come into being until each individual accepts full responsibility for the other" and that each individual charge himself with personal responsibility for the community.[87] Today, Buber charged, youth escapes community responsibility, evades the demands for steadfastness and withdraws into a collective for refuge. In the shelter of the collective the young person pledges allegiance to the group and accepts its common end. He discharges his responsibility for personal decision-making on what is worthy, desired and adequate, and is generally unconcerned whether his ac-tions correspond to his own personal goal which he hoped to achieve. Buber did not object to membership in groups. On the contrary, he greatly favored social dyna-mism. He insisted, however, that at no time should the individual submit blindly to group dogma. He urged youth to refuse to let the power of any slogan coined within the group prevent him from standing up for what is right, for worthy and adequate rather than unworthy and inadequate means. As a responsible person he must fight within the group for what is right and worthwhile. To teach this is the task of the educator.

Buber's humanistic views are particularly evident in his discussion on loss of individuality and personality of youth. Buber complained that an impersonality has been occupying the space between man and man and that a sense of distrust and distance is dominating human lives. Today people are not spontaneous to each other. Man does not consider his fellow man for what he is but as a sum of qualities which are considered for their usefulness, a mere potential prospect for exploitation. But such an attitude turns life into barren soil which destroys all which is organic and constructive. Youth must learn to open up spontaneously to one another, relearn the meaning of personal love and make subject of it so that the innermost of man may live.

Youth's prejudice against faith, asserted Buber, deprives them of one of the great necessities and blessings in life. Here, too, there is reason and perhaps some justification for their attitude. Religious institutions which are supposed to be objective expressions of the reality of faith too often placed themselves in opposition to true faith. Rather than support what is simple, modest and humble in life they sided with those who happened to be powerful and accepted as valid in this world. By their own action these institutions invalidated belief and thus disqualified themselves from representing true faith. Real faith does not mean a profession in a ready-made formula. Rather it is "holding ourselves open to the unconditioned mystery which we encounter in every sphere of our life and which cannot be comprised in any formula."[88] Real faith means readiness to endure life in the face of this mystery and preparedness to live its every facet. True, it is very difficult, at times, but this experience is not new to mankind. Others like our ancient prophets, faced it, engaged their lives to it, and transmitted their encounters to us. Unfortunately, these encounters with faith reach us so often through the conventional form of mechanical religion, yet this need not be so. All man has to do is renew his acquaintance with the life in our Bible, in a free and a loose fashion, so that he "can hear the voice ring forth from the black letters."[89]

The most extreme prejudice of youth, said Buber, is its prejudice against God. This prejudice is not new. Man has exhibited it all through history. Time and again he has proclaimed that God is dead and set out to search for his replacement. But this manifestation is of no import. What man called gods are nothing but images of God who must suffer the fate of images and be broken. In period after period, man has rebelled against his disappointing image and has tried again and again to set up a greater, a more genuine and more just image only to destroy it again when he realized that he failed once more.

Buber taught youth that images indeed topple but he most anxiously wanted them to learn of a mighty and mysterious voice which is never silent. That voice, he taught youth, "speaks in the guise of everything that happens, in the guise of all world events; it speaks to the man of all generations, makes demands upon them, and summons them to accept their responsibility. I have pointed out that it is of the utmost importance not to lose one's openness. But to be open means not to shut out the voice, call it what you will. It does not matter what you call it. All that matters is that you hear it."[90]

Teacher Qualification

BUBER WAS A HUMANIST and a proponent of humanistic education. He considered the teacher's knowledge and skills to be of great importance in the educative process, but his primary concern rested with the attitudinal characteristics and the priority of values of the teacher. His interest was directed at the affective domain which relates to the spiritual qualities of the teacher; his personality, his character, his life objectives, his commitment to scholarship and his educational task, his empathy with his pupils, and his identity with their needs. This domain relates primarily to intelligence, problem solving capacities, behavior, positive self-concept, attitudes, values, self-actualization and discovery of personal conceptions. He believed that these matters of personal and internal meaning constitute the heart and life-stream of education. Although he did not systematically delineate the qualifications of a model teacher, they were quite evident in his writings. He believed that it is the task of the teacher to select the effective world for his students, and as a teacher true to his convictions he indeed selected a certain world which he presented to his pupils through his writings. The characters in his books obviously constitute his models which he hoped his students would emulate. His model teacher was personified in Rabbi Dov Baer, a humanist with existential convictions. He was called the great Maggid (wandering preacher) and embodied the lofty qualities which Buber envisioned in a good teacher.

The Maggid was dedicated to his profession. The teaching task determined the deepest core of his thinking. To him teaching was not an avocation but constituted the major purpose of his life and his way of living.

He was devoted to his pupils. He had a personal concern for the rights, welfare and well-being of each of his disciples. He believed that the fundamental prerequisite for all education is the strength and the tenderness of the relationship between the educator and his pupil.

He handled each of his disciples according to his particular character and his inner destiny.

He upheld the right of his pupils to dissent and respected their freedom of thought and expression. It was said that his students held divergent interpretations of his teachings but he refused to determine which interpretation was authentic, for he believed that each person has the right to interpret truth in his own way.

Buber expected a genuine teacher to emulate the Maggid, who took an existential, non-directive, open-ended approach to education. Like the Maggid, he would expose his pupils to ideas without spinning them out or tying their threads together.

He would guide his pupils to research their own problems independently, or if they so wished, in concert with other pupils.

Like the Maggid, Buber, the genuine teacher, constantly strived to awaken in his pupils the truth which he believed is inherent in the spirit of all people. The teacher must perceive himself not as a dispenser of knowledge and truth, but as a catalyst whose task it is to inspire his students to search and keep searching.

The good teacher must have the will and the ability to pour all the strength of his life into his pupils. He must be the personification of the genuine learning concept. He himself must be the carrier of teaching and the instrument of learning. After his very first visit to the Maggid, one of his disciples said: "When I came before the master, before the Maggid, I saw him on his bed: something was lying there, which was nothing but simple will, the will of the Most High." On that, Buber commented: "That is why his disciples learned even more and greater things from his sheer being than from his words."[91]

The ideal teacher must assist his pupil not only with his intellectual needs, the domain of his soul, but also with his ordinary daily cares, the griefs and despairs of life itself, "and if these are not dealt with, how shall those loftier concerns be approached?" The ideal teacher must teach his pupil how to conduct his affairs so that his soul remains free, and he must teach his pupil to strengthen his soul to keep him steadfast beneath the blows of destiny. The teacher must take the pupil by the hand and guide him until he is able to venture on alone. He does not relieve him until he has grown strong enough to do for himself.[92]

The master teacher, like the Hasidic Zaddik (sage), must come down to the level of his pupils and mix with them in order to raise them to the rung of their individual perfection. Buber quoted the Baal Shem Tov saying: "If a man falls into the mire and his friend wants to fetch him out, he must not hesitate to get himself a little dirty."[93]

Good teaching is reciprocal. "The teacher helps his disciples find themselves, and in hours of desolation, the disciples help their teacher find himself again. The teacher kindles the souls of his disciples and they surround him and light his life with the flame he has kindled."[94]

Buber's model teacher, like the Maggid, is not a professional teacher as we know him today, but resembled instead the classical old "master," who did not treat education just as a profession. The journeyman or the apprentice lived with him and learned all just by being in his presence. They learned from him through his direct teaching and by observing him. They learned from his handiwork and from his brain work. They learned through osmosis. They received his spirit. A hidden influence proceeded from his integrity as an integrating force.[95]

Buber's philosophy is that genuine education is not achieved through prescription but by example. What counts in education more than content and educational strategy is the quality, integrity, sincerity and commitment of the teacher, his identity with his pupils and his ability to see the world from the pupil's point of view. Buber knew that we could not return to the old master as a model for modern education. He hoped, however, that we might recapture as much as possible of the master's spirit and adapt it to modern day education.

Buber held that the master teacher must possess such exceptional guidance and counseling skills which enable him to establish and strengthen in his disciples the yearning for personal unity, from which the unity of mankind should be born.[96] He must also aim to establish peace within the student, for "only when man establishes peace within himself," Buber quoted Simha Bunem of Pzycha, "is he capable of establishing it in the world."[97]

He also held that the teacher must be a leader, albeit, a special kind of a teacher. He maintained that "it is not the aim that there should be only leaders and no followers anymore; that would be more utopian than any utopia. The aim is that the leaders should remain leaders and not become dominating rulers. More precisely stated, they should assume only those elements of domination which are necessarily demanded by the circumstance."[98]

Genuine teaching is not a mere profession, like engineering or accounting where mastery of skills suffice. The educator, more than anyone else must stand in the service of truth while leading. Putting it in Buber's words: "We call that man a teacher of all people who recognizes both eternal truth and present reality; that man who measures one through the other."[99]

Another quality of a good teacher is that he is a man who acts, and acts adequately. The core of his teaching is this: he lets his students participate in his life, and so he lets them grasp the search of action.[100]

Buber viewed with dissatisfaction highly structured and strictly directed instruction which became the teaching mode of his time, and lamented that intentional education has irrevocably won the day; we can no more retrogress regarding the reality of the school than we can regarding the reality of technology.[101] The teacher, in his opinion, must be able to progress into the "transhumanification" of reality rather than into mechanistic instruction. The humanistic teacher must act not through dictation but "as if he were not doing it." He must act subtly, by the lifting of a finger and through a questioning

79

glance. He must teach "as if" he were not teaching. This could be achieved by the master teacher who knows how to gain the trust of his student. Through the genuine teacher the student learns to trust the world because there is such a man (as the teacher); this is the innermost work of educational relationship. While there is such a man, the chaotic cannot be the true truth. Surely there is a light in the darkness, and redemption in terror. Great love is hidden in the dullness of coexistence.[102] To gain the students' trust is not an easy task, yet this is the task of the genuine teacher.

Buber knew that one of the educational tasks is to discipline the student, but he rejected the conventional extrinsic mode. His view on discipline could be readily extracted from his Hasidic parable which he related in his spiritual master, the Baal Shem Tov.

One late afternoon a man whom no one knew arrived in a small Jewish village and set out to remedy the souls of the people with moral and ethical tales and stories of hope and redemption. Soon a whole group of people gathered about the story teller and still their numbers grew. So absorbed were the people in his stories that they forgot to go to the synagogue for the evening prayer. The Rabbi of the synagogue, a strict and harsh person who was quick to fly into temper, angrily summoned the stranger, who later became known as the Baal Shem Tov, the great luminary of the Hasidic movement, to appear before him. "What are you doing!" shouted the Rabbi, "keeping the people from prayer!"

"Rabbi," said the Baal Shem Tov calmly, "It does not become you to fly into a rage. Rather let me tell you a story."

"What do you think you are doing!" was what the

Rabbi wanted to repeat, and then he looked at the man closely for the first time. It is true that he immediately turned his eyes away, nevertheless the words he had been about to say stuck in his throat. The Baal Shem had begun his story, and the Rabbi had to listen like all the others.

"Once I drove cross-country with three horses," said the Baal Shem, "a bay, a piebald, and a white horse. And not one of the three horses would neigh. Then I met a peasant coming toward me and he called: 'slacken the reins!' So I slackened the reins, and then all three horses began to neigh." The Rabbi could say nothing for emotion. "Three," the Baal Shem repeated. "Bay, piebald and white did not neigh. The peasant knew what to do; slacken reins—and they neighed." The Rabbi bowed his head in silence. "The peasant gave good advice," said the Baal Shem. "Do you understand?" "I understand," answered the Rabbi and burst into tears.[103]

Moral Education

BUBER WAS A MORAL PHILOSOPHER. Friends and opponents viewed him as the great exponent, indeed the personification of the loftiest moral and ethical values, and expected him to propose a moral system to guide man, yet he never acknowledged a framework of laws and prescriptions, nor did he offer a system of ethics of his own. His close friend Hugo Bergman voiced reproach when he said: "of a teacher we expect that he will give indication as to how we should walk the way,"[104] nevertheless, Buber refused to offer a moral system, insisting that by so doing he would injure the core of his views. In this respect he acted like his mentor, the great Hasidic teacher, Rabbi Bunam Von Prsysucha who once said to his students: "I wanted to write a book called Adam, which would be about the whole man, but then I decided not to write it."[105] Buber explained that Rabbi Bunam, like many other great men, knew that this subject is most deserving of study, yet he also knew the magnitude and the complexities of this task.[106] Similarly, Buber knew that man is in search of a moral system which would remove from him all insecurity, all unrest about meaning, all terror of decision, all abysmal problems, but like Rabbi Bunam he not only declined but vociferously opposed these expectations and indeed refused to offer such a system of ethics. He claimed that he did not even know

82

of the existence of such a universal valid system. He was an existentialist who believed that all a teacher can do for his students is no more than "point the way" and merely give direction, but not prescribe the manner in which one should strive for that direction. He believed that each student must personally discover and independently acquire for himself the best moral decision applicable for a given situation at a given time.[107]

Although Buber refused to prescribe a moral system, he extensively addressed himself on the subject of values. A study of his writings indeed reveals a moral philosophy.

Buber's moral philosophy is based upon several basic assumptions. The cornerstone of his assumptions is his belief that there is in reality an absolute Supreme Being, namely, God. He held that "over and above all the countless and varied peoples there is an authority . . . to which communities as well as individuals must inwardly render an account of themselves."[108] This absolute authority is the source of all values and moral obligations. He insisted that moral values are not derived from man's social or natural environment, as was claimed by John Dewey, but from the existing absolute Supreme Being to whom man is accountable. Said Buber: "I am constitutionally incapable of convincing of myself as the ultimate source of moral approval or disapproval of myself, as surely for the absoluteness that I to be sure do not possess, but nevertheless imply with respect to this yes or no. The encounter with the original voice, the original source of yes or no cannot be replaced by any self encounter."[109] Only God is the source of all values and only in relationship to God can man discover true values, because "only an absolute can give the quality of absoluteness to an obligation."[110]

Man, insisted Buber, is not endowed with the power to invent values, he can only discover the absolute values which are in existence.

This does not handicap man; on the contrary, this is to his advantage. Had man possessed the arbitrary power to make values, he would also be able to unmake them, and consequently be bound to no values at all, which will lead to inevitable human decadence and ultimate destruction of humanity. Buber explained that "one can believe in and accept a meaning or a value, one can set it as a guiding light over one's life if one has discovered it, not if one has invented it . . . not if I have freely chosen it for myself from among the existing possibilities and perhaps have in addition decided with one fellow creature: this shall be valid from now on."[111] Moral values, then, are absolutely valid and are related to an absolute. That absolute exists and he is the source of all values and moral obligations, and to him is man accountable. Man cannot invent values, he merely discovers them. This discovery is made in a simple, yet a unique way, which Buber calls revelation.

Revelation, the second basic assumption in Buber's moral philosophy, is not a supernatural phenomenon, nor is it a spectacular occurrence which is accompanied by thunder and lightning on a desert mountain which is covered with fire and smoke. It is a simple phenomenon, present here and now, yet primal, and penetrating. To Buber, revelation means a simple everyday, authentic meeting between man and God, yet, a meeting of such great impact that it transforms man into a new being, one who is truly human. "What is the eternal, primal phenomenon, present here and now, of that which we term revelation?", asked Buber rhetorically. "It is the phenomenon," he said, "that a man does not pass, from the moment of the supreme meeting, the same being as he enters it, rather, in that moment something happens to man. At times it is like a light breath, at times like a wrestling bout, but always it happens. The man who emerges from the act of pure relation that so involves his being has now in his being something more that has grown in him, of which he did not know before and whose origin he is not rightly able to indicate."[112]

Revelation, then, is what gives man an inner light and insight into new situations, and helps him become truly human. Revelation is indeed an encounter between man and his God, yet, it is not a phenomenon which the ordinary man cannot attain. Every man can experience revelation, and every moment in human existence is a possible moment for revelation. All that man has to do in order to experience revelation is to listen carefully to the voice which addresses him. He only needs to "listen to that which the voice, sounding forth from this ever wishes to communicate to him, its witness, to his constitution, to life, to his sense of duty."[113] When man truly reaches out for revelation man is capable of experiencing revelation. Through revelation he confronts the absolute and through revelation he is able to discover absolute moral values.

Moral values, according to Buber, are indeed absolute and divinely inspired, yet, he claimed, moral values are not given to man as a system of ethics nor as a codex of laws. "The revelation does not pour itself into the world through him who receives it as through a funnel," said Buber, "it comes to him and seizes his whole elemental being in all its particular nature, and fuses with it. The man, too, who is the 'mouth' of the revelation, is indeed this, not a speaking-tube or any kind of instrument, but an organ, which sounds according to its own laws; and to sound means to modify."[114]

Revelation of values, then, does not mean the imposition of moral laws upon man; it only means the exposure of universal values to man's scrutiny. Similarly, the absolute does not yield a clear and certain moral system. "God has truth" explained Buber, "but he does not have a system. He expressed his truth through his will, but his will is not a program."[115] In short, there is no system of values, nor is man certain to experience revelation. How, then, can man find his answers to his perplexities about right and wrong? How can he, who truly desires a moral life, find his way in his perplexed existence?

This brings us to the third assumption in Buber's moral philosophy: to the concept which Buber calls the "narrow ridge."

Like all other existentialists Buber insisted that Reality is "self-operating in cosmos of choice." Man, by his nature is destined to a life of constant choice, and with every choice he casts a ballot as to what is becoming. This is not a handicap, but indeed an exclusive privilege of man. No other worldly creature is endowed with such a gift. This privilege, however, saddles man with the heaviness of awesome responsibilities. The human predicament is that he must walk his entire life a "narrow ridge" of constant choice. Man has no one to turn to, save himself, to find a better life. "I do not believe that revelation is ever a formulation of a law," said Buber, "it is only through man in his self-contradiction that revelation becomes legislation. This is the fact of man."[116]

The fact of man is that each person must discover and acquire for himself in a work that demands of him the best possibilities of his soul.

The right and the obligation of each person to make his own decision of what is right and wrong poses a serious problem. Is each man's claim for revelation valid? Is each person capable of catching a glimpse of the appearance of the Absolute?

Buber himself realized this problem when he wrote that "the question of questions which takes precedence over every other is: are you really addressed by the Absolute or by one of his apes? . . . in our age especially it appears to be extremely difficult to distinguish the one from the other."[117] How can we indeed distinguish between the true and the false without reliable criteria? How can each person be his own judge?

Buber agreed that to know the right way is never a simple matter. He recognized that every person who has ever labored over the question of what is good and what is evil knows how hard it is to find the right way. He also knew that "there is not the slightest assurance that our decision is right in any way but a personal way."[118] Life is a chain of uncertainties and all our decisions must be made in the light of what each particular circumstance demands of us. Our worldly lot is to run a risk of decision in every step of our lives. Every moral and ethical person "knows that he cannot objectively and reliably know whether that which he intends to do is the correct answer to the problem presented to him."[119] Our lot is to live through these moments daringly, in fear and trembling. We have just one saving grace: to align ourselves with God and aspire for His revelation. A person who does that is indeed fortunate because in such a person "the human substance is melted by the spiritual fire which visits him, and there now breaks forth from it a word, a statement, which is human in its meaning and form, human conception and human speech, and yet witnesses to Him who stimulated it and to His will."[120] There are no long-established rules of behavior to lead us in the intricacies of life, but a bond with God makes us ever aware of our responsibilities and renders us fruitful.

What, then, shall we do with the criminal who may be acting in accordance with what he believes is the voice of God? Buber insisted that this hypothetical instance is absurd, just as the claim of a mad man that he is God is absurd, because "a man who is not mad can only believe that he is following the voice of God if he acts with his whole soul, i.e., if out of its corner no demonic whisper penetrates to his open ears."[121] Buber insisted that one cannot do evil with his whole soul, i.e., one can only do it through holding down forcibly the forces striving against it.

A problem also exists in regard to moral education. If moral judgements are subjective to each person, and if man can make moral decisions only in the light of the uniqueness of each particular circumstance, what is there to teach youth in moral education? Buber believed that the major task of the educator is to educate his pupil in correct thinking until he becomes able to recognize the decadent concepts which surround him. He must also help his pupil to weigh carefully the alternatives in each situation. Finally, he must guide his student to select those views which are well founded on human reality.[122] The major task of education is to make each student aware of his responsibility to search, research and become uniquely himself. Putting it in Buber's own words:

"In decision, taking the direction thus means: taking the direction toward the point of being at which, executing for my part the design which I am, I encounter the divine myself on my created uniqueness, the mystery waiting for me . . . every revelation is revelation of human service to the goal of creation, in which service man authenti-cates himself."[123] All the student can do and must do is "authenticate" himself. In this respect the Hasidic tale which Buber recorded in his writings is most demonstra-tive of his position: "Before his death, Rabbi Zusya said: 'In the coming world, they will not ask me: why were you not Moses? They will ask me: Why were you not Zusya?' "[124] The task of education is to make the student aware that he must become uniquely himself and by so doing he will be moving in the direction of God and his values.

National Education

TODAY, BUBER'S CONCEPTS ON EDUCATION are more pertinent than ever before. With the advent of science and technology, our world became a global village. Distant lands are bridged by jet planes and space ships bring remote planets into man's testing sphere. Today, all people are aware, as never before, that man is not an island unto himself and that no people goes unaffected by others. As we look at our ecological environment we quickly realize that famine has no national boundaries, plagues travel from country to country without a passport and pollution endangers the lives of our entire global population without distinction. As we look at our political map we note with alarm how one skirmish is capable of embroiling us all in a world catastrophe and that our problems are of mankind magnitude and require global solutions. Modern educators, alarmed by the impending holocaust, came to believe that the solution for most of our problems can be found only within the framework of a supernational design. We came to realize that no single nation or small group of nations can abolish war; no single industry or group of industries can deal effectively with malnutrition or world productivity; and that no private or public agency can deal with starvation, population growth, health, pollution, or drought. The issues which we face today are panhuman and supernational, and the only potential power which is capable of embracing our problems, deriving reasonable solutions, and implementing them is the totality of our mankind society.[125]

Similarly, Buber believed that our personal and national goals can no longer be limited to personal freedom and national freedom. He believed that we must shift from our fragmentary existence into a whole and unified way of life not only for ourselves but for our entire world civilization. We must teach our children to strive toward a supernational task, namely toward universal humanism. Education must aim to convert this supernational task into a living urge, into a vital personal endeavor and creative power. It must incorporate social truth in the lives of individuals living with one another and translate the idea of true community into reality. It must teach our children to favor justice over instinctive egoism and to strive for a messianic climate throughout our world. Free nations and national movements which strive for liberation must make their youth conscious of the great spiritual values whose source is in the origin of their people, and deliberately weave these values into the design of their lives.[126] Today education can no longer foster merely the individual's self-fulfillment and the welfare of his country. A new curriculum must be developed; a curriculum which will perceive all mankind as a unitary whole. This curriculum must teach students to transcend their selves and their national welfare and learn to integrate themselves with their families, with their immediate society, with their nation and with mankind at large. The nature of education must be of great concern to all nations but particularly to newly emerging nations. Only recently many nations, European and

91

African, overthrew the yoke of imperialism, reached independence and are now struggling for self actualization. Until now national independence has been the prime goal and objective of these movements. Now these nations stand on the crossroad between creativity and convention, between a world-receptive human attitude and sterile egoism. Education, being a potent agent in this choice, calls for a careful analysis of its role and responsibilities. In this context Buber's views on national education merit serious consideration.

Buber devoted a whole essay to national education.[127] In it he carefully analyzed the role of nations in seas of turmoil and tranquility and masterfully offered a humanistic design which he hoped would lead to universal equitability and harmony. He recognized that education is not a static invariable, and that its role and functions change with the changes in its environment. He observed that the patterns familiar to us from history point at two basic approaches to education which correspond to two basic types of environment. In tranquil days, during periods of genuine and vigorous culture, education does not impose nor is it arbitrary, but draws out of the pupil that which is in him. In such days education assumes the role of a gardener who "fertilizes and waters the soil, prunes and props the young plant, and removes the rank weed from around it. But after he has done all this, if the weather is propitious, he trusts to the natural growth of that which is inherent in the seed."[128]

In such an era education holds that man is good and that the characteristics of each individual are predetermined by his innate endowment. This type of education is humble and passive. Like the gardener it acts as a facilitator. It merely fosters the natural process of the

92

pupil's growth to reach his culmination. It allows full scope to the pupil's individualism and to his personal differences.[129]

On the other hand, during turbulent days, when cultural productivity declines, education arbitrarily shapes the pupil into a predetermined form which aims to satisfy immediate situational needs. In this approach education means shaping the pupil into a form which the educators predetermine. It aims to influence the pupil's soul and develop him in accordance to what the educator deems right. In this system the educator regards man as a creature with plastic and educable potentialities which empower him to mold and shape his pupil in his own image.[130] This approach is that of a sculptor. "Like Michelangelo he sometimes sees the shape hidden in the crude marble, but it is the image which exists in his soul which guides him in working on the block, and which he wishes to realize in the material at his disposal."[131]

It is apparent that different societal patterns foster different ideals, but what determines these ideals?

The patterns familiar to us throughout history signify that during periods of genuine and vigorous enlightenment, social ideals were never determined arbitrarily. They emerged from the people themselves, reflecting the spirit and the will of their society. These ideals were not personal. The culture itself produced a pattern which was the basis of its community life and was accepted by everyone as the supreme and authoritative modus vivendi of that particular civilization at that particular time. The ideals expressed all facets of that community, its character and its aspirations. Sometimes these ideals reflected the image of a single nation and at other times they embraced a number of nations. In all cases, however, they expressed the deepest life, character and de-sires of their entire society. Educators were not obliged to superimpose their personal ideas on their students. They merely gave their pupils access to the proper sub-ject matter and provided them with the proper facilities for practice. The rest they trusted to the natural growth of that which was inherent in the pupil. The goals of the community became the goals of education.

From history we also learned that during days of stress and turmoil, when cultural productivity declined and intellectual tradition disintegrated, the ideal pattern which gave full scope to the individualism of man ceased to exist. In such an epoch the ideal pattern no longer emerged from its growing civilization. It sprang from the unique historical situation in which the community found itself and wished to overcome; situations such as the movements in behalf of national liberation which strove for national rebirth and fought for freedom. These movements realized the necessity of rearing a type of human being who was willing and able to perform a singular historical feat, that of liberating his nation. In such an era, education was governed by legitimate spiritual and historical needs, even though its purposes and contents were decided by convention.

Buber cautioned, however, that the justification for such a situational ideal persists only until its task has been achieved, but when the nation has won its independence it loses its situational purpose. At this point, if education does not wish to deteriorate into na-tionalistic convention, it must set for itself a greater pur-pose, namely, universal humanism and panhuman values. This objective, Buber believed, is not hard to reach. He explained that great national movements always contain the germ of humanism within themselves and that the task of education is to develop this germ. He cautioned, however, against nationalistic education and stated that "nationalistic convention which regards itself as a supreme triumph of national education is its death."[132]

Buber's message has, of course, universal significance and could serve as a challenge to all emerging nations. His apocalyptic fervor was directed, however, at his own people, Israel. During the first half of the present century he saw his fellow Jews begin their return to their ancestral home and observed with gratitude and admiration the revival of Israel as a nation in its ancient homeland. At the same time, he viewed with concern the possibility of its becoming a chauvinistic society which could negate the purpose of its existence. He proclaimed emphatically that "the prophets of Israel, more than anyone else in the history of the human spirit, express the truth that a people does not exist for its own sake, that its historic mission is to act upon its fellow nation in accordance with the task it assumed, that of 'being a blessing' . . . Leaders of great national movements have taken this prophetic law to heart and made it the basic law of national education."[133]

Why must Israel, more than any other nation, conduct its life on the highest moral and ethical level? Why must Israel, above all nations, strive to live as a model society, eternally striving for panhuman justice and supernational humanity?

The answer, explained Buber, lies in the reason why ancient Israel was established as a people and a nation and the purpose for its existence through the ages. The supernational task was not imposed upon Israel at a late period in its history; its distinctiveness as a just society was an integral part of its past. The prophets of old warned that unless Israel fulfilled the commandment to establish an ethical society during the era of its independence, it would have to go into exile and there learn what is just and what is unjust. But if Israel should return to its ancestral land and practice genuine justice, true humanity and international peace would issue forth from the mountain of Zion. Modern emancipated Israel has, thus, a peculiar mission. It must foster a new type of person who will, hopefully, achieve his people's mission: to serve as an architect and builder of a panhuman, moral, and ethical society. The war for Israel's liberation had a greater intent than throwing off an alien yoke. The purpose was to transform the entire life of the people. "The goal (was) a regeneration of the very being; it (was) an inner renewal, a rescue from physical and spiritual deterioration, the turning from a fragmentary, contradictory existence to a whole and unified way of life; it (was) purification and redemption."[134] Of course, the survival of Israel was a necessary premise, but it did not survive for the sake of surviving. It survived to achieve its universal task. The task of education is, therefore, to inspire individuals who will hopefully become independent and responsive beings and will strive for a new humanism. "National education," concluded Buber, "is the way that leads to the fulfillment of Judaism; nationalistic education is the way that leads to dejudaization under a Jewish banner."[135]

Buber knew that a mere theory of his humanistic concept would not suffice to enhance his position, and selected from the active Israeli society a living model of his new type of man, the Halutz, the modern Israeli pioneer. He saw in the Halutz the embodiment of his ideal characteristics, and in him he recognized the personification of the union of national and social elements. He pointed out that the Halutz demonstrated a desire to contribute personally through his own labor to the rebirth of his people in their own land. He dedicated his entire life to labor. He participated in the upbuilding of his homeland as a laborer only, not as one who directs the work of others. Through his personal action, he helped to establish a working society, a social synthesis of people, land and labor. He personally participated in the formation of a human community—a union of persons who live together, work together—a union which is established on just relations of all to all. He was imbued with the desire "to incorporate social truth in the life of individuals living with one another, the longing to translate the idea of true community into reality."[136]

The Halutz is not a product of the Western world, nor is he the offspring of occidental socialism. "He is animated by the age old longing to incorporate social truth in the life of individuals living with one another, the longing to translate the idea of a true community into reality."[137] He is not the unfolding of biological and historical developments. He evolves from a people who made a decision a long time ago to favor justice over egoism, and promote panhuman principles and messianic values.

Buber believed that the goal of national education is to set a pattern for this type of man, a man who can translate ideas into life and satisfy the longing for a just communal existence. He believed that its task is to bring to the attention of youth the great spiritual values whose source is the origin of their people and weave it into their lives.

Bibliographical Notes

1. Howard Morley Sacher, The Course of Modern Jewish History (New York: A Delta Book, 1958), p. 74.
2. Ibid., pp. 76-77.
3. Ibid., pp. 199-201.
4. George F. Kneller, Existentialism and Education (New York: Wiley & Sons, Inc., 1958), pp. 6-12.
5. Ibid., p. 3.
6. Ibid., p. 13.
7. Ibid.,
8. Ibid., p. 9.
9. Ibid., p. 114.
10. Ibid., p. 129.
11. Ibid., p. 13.
12. Ibid., p. 75.
13. Ibid., p. 72.
14. Ibid., p. 78.
15. Sachar, op. cit. p. 264.
16. Ibid.,
17. Max I. Dimont, Jews, God and History (New York: Simon and Schuster, 1962), p. 398.
18. Leon Simon, Selected Essays of Ahad Ha-Am (New York: Antheneum 1970).
19. Dimont, op. cit. p. 347.
20. Aubrey Hodes, Martin Buber (New York: Viking Press, 1971), p. 146.
21. Martin Buber, Besod Siach (Jerusalem: Mosad Bialik 1973), Introduction by Hugo Bergman.
22. S. H. Bergman, Besod Siach (Jerusalem: Mosad Bialik, 1973), pp. 14-15.
23. Victor Frankel, Man's Search for Meaning (Boston: Beacon Press, 1963), p. 69.
24. Paul Arthur Schilpp and Maurice Friedman, editors, The Philosophy of Martin Buber, (London: Cambridge University Press, 1967), p. 10.
25. Martin Buber, I and Thou (New York: Charles Scribner's Sons, 1958), p. 14.

26. Ibid., p. 8.
27. Ibid, p. 62.
28. Ibid., pp. 9-10.
29. Martin Buber, Besod Siach op. cit. p. 34.
30. Ibid., p. 43.
31. Van Cleve Morris, Existentialism and Education, appearing in Joe Park, editor Selected Readings in the Philosophy of Education, Third edition (New York: Macmillan, 1970), p. 314.
32. Max Arzt, Justice and Mercy (New York: Holt, Rinehart and Winston, 1963), p. 65.
33. Ibid.
34. Martin Buber, Between Man and Man (New York: Macmillan Co. 1971), p. 83.
35. Ibid., p. 87.
36. Ibid., p. 88.
37. Ibid., p. 98.
38. Ibid., p. 87.
39. Ibid., p. 99.
40. Kurzweil, Buber on Education, p. 225.
41. Buber, Between Man and Man, op. cit. pp. 5-6.
42. Ibid., p. 100.
43. Ibid., p. 101.
44. Martin Buber, Israel and the World (New York: Schocken Books, 1963), p. 138.
45. Ibid.
46. Jerusalem Talmud, Shabbat, p. 36.
47. Buber, Israel and the World, op. cit. pp. 140-142.
48. op. cit. p. 142.
49. op. cit. p. 144.
50. Talmud. Kiddushin, p. 40b.
51. Buber, Israel and the World, op. cit. p. 145.
52. Buber, Between Man and Man, op. cit. p. 105.
53. Ibid., p.
54. Ibid., pp. 103-108.
55. Ibid, p. 111.
56. Ibid.
57. Ibid., p. 112.
58. Ibid., p. 113.
59. Ibid., p. 114.
60. Ibid.
61. Ibid., p. 115.
62. Ibid., p. 116.
63. Ibid., p. 117.
64. Martin Buber, "Chinuch Mevugarim", Molad (1950) Vol. 23-24, No. 4, p. 301.
65. Buber "Adult Education in Israel" The Torch (1952), p. 7.
66. Buber, "Chinuch Mevugarim" op. cit.

67. Buber, "Adult Education in Israel" op. cit.
68. Buber, "Chinuch Mevugarim" op. cit., p. 30.
69. Ibid.
70. Ibid., p. 302.
71. Ibid., p. 303.
72. Aubrey Hodes, op. cit., p. 117.
73. Buber, "Chinuch Mevugarim" op. cit., p. 298.
74. Ibid.
75. Ibid.
76. Ibid., p. 299.
77. Ibid.
78. Ibid., p. 302.
79. Ibid., p. 299.
80. Ibid., p. 303.
81. Ibid.
82. Martin Buber, Between Man and Man, (New York: Macmillan Co., 1971), p. 107.
83. Martin Buber, Israel and the World, (New York: Schocken Books, 1963), p. 42.
84. Ibid., p. 41.
85. Ibid., p. 45-46.
86. George F. Kneller, Existentialism and Education (New York: Wiley and Sons Inc., 1958), p. 16.
87. Buber, Israel and the World, op. cit., p. 87.
88. Ibid., p. 49.
89. Ibid., p. 50.
90. Ibid., p. 51.
91. Buber, Between Man and Man, op. cit., pp. 16-17.
92. Martin Buber, Tales of the Hasidim (New York: The Commentary Classics, 1958), p. 5.
93. Ibid., p. 7.
94. Ibid., p. 8.
95. Buber, Between Man and Man, op. cit., p. 90.
96. Ibid., p. 116.
97. Buber, Tales of the Hasidim, op. cit., p. 264.
98. Martin Buber, Pfade in Utopie (Heidelberg: Verlag Lambert Schneider, p. 177.
99. Martin Buber, Kampf um Israel, Reden und Aufsatze, (Berlin: Schocken Verlag, 1921-1932), p. 152.
100. Buber, Between Man and Man, op. cit., p. 89.
101. Ibid., p. 90.
102. Ibid., p. 98.
103. Buber, Tales of the Hasidim, op. cit., p. 57.
104. Paul Arthur Schilpp and Maurice Friedman, editors, The Philosophy of Martin Buber, (London: Cambridge University Press, 1967), p. 717.
105. Buber, Between Man and Man, op. cit. p. 118.

101

106. Ibid., p. 139.
107. Schilpp and Friedman, The Philosophy of Martin Buber, op. cit., p. 718.
108. Buber, Israel and the World, op. cit., p. 220.
109. Martin Buber, Eclipse of God, (New York: Harper Torchbook, 1957), p. 98.
110. Ibid., p. 18.
111. Buber, Between Man and Man., op. cit., p. 108.
112. Buber, I and Thou, op. cit., p. 109.
113. Buber, Israel and the World, op. cit., p. 98.
114. Buber, I and Thou, op. cit., p. 117.
115. Buber, Israel and the World, op. cit., p. 114.
116. Nahum N. Glatzer, editor, Franz Rosenzweig On Jewish Learning, (New York: Shocken 1955), p. 111.
117. Buber, Eclipse of God, op. cit., p. 118.
118. Buber, Between Man and Man, op. cit., p. 69.
119. Buber, Tales of the Hasidim, op. cit., p. 162.
120. Buber, Eclipse of God, op. cit., p. 135.
121. Schilpp and Friedman, The Philosophy of Martin Buber, op. cit., p. 720.
122. Buber, "Chinuch Mevugarim," op. cit., p. 297.
123. Martin Buber, Good and Evil, (New York: Charles Scribner's sons, 1953), p. 142.
124. Buber, Tales of the Hasidim, op. cit., p. 251.
125. John Goodlad, Toward a Mankind School, (Los Angeles: The Council for the Study of Mankind—unpublished manuscript), p. iv.
126. Buber, Israel and the World, op. cit., p. 149.
127. Israel and the World, op. cit., pp. 149-163.
128. Ibid., p. 149.
129. Ibid., p. 150.
130. Ibid.
131. Ibid., p. 149
132. Ibid., p. 155.
133. Ibid., p. 154.
134. Ibid., p. 157.
135. Ibid.
136. Ibid., p. 158.
137. Ibid.